THE REAL VOICE

"THINGS GET VERY LONELY IN WASHINGTON SOMETIMES. THE REAL VOICE OF THE GREAT PEOPLE OF AMERICA SOMETIMES SOUNDS FAINT AND DISTANT IN THAT STRANGE CITY."

—WOODROW WILSON

THE REAL VOICE

by Richard Harris

THE MACMILLAN COMPANY, NEW YORK
COLLIER-MACMILLAN LIMITED, LONDON

Second Printing, 1964

The Macmillan Company, New York
Collier-Macmillan Canada Ltd., Toronto, Ontario

Library of Congress catalog card number: 64-20456
Printed in the United States of America

Most of the contents of this book appeared in *The New Yorker*, in somewhat different form.

ACKNOWLEDGMENT

A great many people contributed to this book. Naturally, some of them prefer to remain anonymous, and since it would slight their part to name only the others, I shall leave it at that. However, I would like to thank all of them, along with those members of *The New Yorker* and the Macmillan staffs who helped make the book what it is.

Most of all, I would like to express my gratitude to the late Senator Estes Kefauver. A year or so before he died, he decided to let me in on what he called "the ins and outs, the ups and downs, and the dirty dealings" that characterized the three years he spent in trying to get an effective drug bill through Congress. Without his coöperation, this would have been a different story.

CONTENTS

Part One. THE INVESTIGATION

I One rainy, cold morning early in February of 1951, Walton Hamilton, a Washington attorney, awoke in his home in Arlington, Virginia, with a severely inflamed throat. That afternoon, he went to see his physician, who told him that he was suffering from a virulent streptococcic infection, and prescribed one of the new "wonder" drugs—an antibiotic called Chloromycetin. Stopping at a drugstore on his way home, Hamilton learned that Chloromycetin cost fifty cents a pill. For a good many years, he had suspected that doctors in general had little idea of the prices that their patients had to pay for medicine, and he was outraged at this particular price—eight dollars for a four-day supply of the drug—so then and there he telephoned his own doctor to ask if some cheaper medication wouldn't do. The physician, admitting that he had had no idea of the cost of Chloromycetin, said that either of two other new antibiotics—Aureomycin or Terramycin—would be suitable, and he promised to check on their prices and call Hamilton back.

A few minutes later, he did. "I'm sorry, but they're all the same price," he reported.

"Exactly the same?" Hamilton asked.

"To the penny."

"I presume they're all made by the same company, then," Hamilton said.

"No," the doctor replied. "They're made by three different companies."

Hamilton bought Chloromycetin.

That evening, Hamilton described his pharmaceutical adventures to his wife—Dr. Irene Till, who was then working part time for the Federal Trade Commission as an industrial economist—and they came to the conclusion that the similarity of prices was worth examining. All in all, they were in a better position than the average couple to get something done. Hamilton, formerly a professor of law at Yale, had served as a consultant to the Antitrust Division of the Department of Justice when it was headed by Thurman Arnold, one of the celebrated trustbusters of the New Deal era, and was now a partner in his former boss's law firm—Arnold, Fortas & Porter. Price-fixing and other violations of the antitrust laws are the concern of both the F.T.C. and the Justice Department, but Hamilton felt that the Commission afforded the better line of approach, since at the time it had the discretionary power to issue subpoenas and the Justice Department did not.

The first thing next day, Dr. Till discussed her husband's experience with her immediate superior, Dr. John M. Blair, chief of the F.T.C.'s Division of Economic Reports. Dr. Blair (like Dr. Till, a Ph.D., not an M.D.) thought the matter over, agreed that it merited an official examination, and formally recommended that the Commission make a preliminary study. Shortly afterward, a couple of investigators were assigned to look into the matter, but it appears that they didn't look into it very deeply. An attorney who was then fairly high up in the F.T.C. hierarchy later explained, "For some reason, the Commission decided not to issue any subpoenas, and the investigators got the runaround. In essence, what happened was that they went to the officers of various drug corporations and asked, 'Are you conspiring to fix prices?' When everyone answered, 'Who *us?*' the investigators came back and recommended that the file be closed. It was."

Some members of the F.T.C. staff kept hoping that one day the file would be reopened. But then, in 1953, after the change of administration, the Commission was rocked so violently that a good part of the crew went overboard. The new chairman was a Washington lawyer named Edward F. Howrey, and not long after he took over, he made a speech before the New York State Bar Association in which he promised vigorous enforcement of the antitrust laws and noted that this would depend in large measure upon the work of his economists. However, the Select Committee on Small Business of the House of Representatives later reported that Howrey had "failed to inform his audience that under his direction there had been a reduction in force at the F.T.C. . . . with its greatest impact against the staff of F.T.C. economists." The report continued, "Only nine economists remained unaffected. Thirteen had been separated, another had resigned while facing separation, and four had been demoted and reassigned." Dr. Till was cashiered, while Blair was demoted and more or less put on the shelf. So, it appeared, was any plan for investigating the drug industry.

At about this time, Senator Warren G. Magnuson, a Democrat from Washington, began to grow curious about the high prices of drugs—particularly the newer ones. As a member of the Labor, Health, Education, and Welfare Subcommittee of the Senate Appropriations Committee, he had learned that drugs represented a major expense in federal and joint federal-and-state welfare programs. "Back in the early fifties, I started getting a lot of complaints from elderly constituents about drug prices," he has said. "I looked into the matter, and found that some pensioners spent as much as a third of their income for medication. A little later, I was in Sweden, and I happened to notice that some American-made drugs cost only twenty per cent of what they cost here —American-made drugs, mind you."

In 1955, control of Congress passed to the Democrats, and control of the Senate Independent Offices Appropriations Subcommittee, which holds hearings on the annual budgets of the federal regulatory agencies, passed to Senator Magnuson. In May of that year, when Howrey appeared before the subcommittee to defend the F.T.C.'s request for a budget of $4,300,000 for the next fiscal year, Magnuson brought up the prices of antibiotics, saying that an investigation might show "markups running to four hundred and five hundred per cent of the cost of production," and adding that he thought the field would be a good one for the F.T.C. to study. Howrey agreed, "Your views count with us," he said. "We will begin the antibiotic studies as soon as we can." A year later, when the F.T.C. again appeared before the subcommittee to defend its budget—represented this time by a new chairman, John W. Gwynne, a former Republican congressman from Iowa—Magnuson asked how the antibiotics study was progressing. Gwynne answered that at the moment the Commission was shorthanded but that the study would probably be ready by the summer of 1957. At Gwynne's next appearance before the subcommittee, in April, 1957, Magnuson again mentioned the report, remarking, "I was wondering how you were coming along on that." This time Gwynne was more definite. "We hope to have it in the hands of the printer by June 30th," he said.

II A few months earlier, another senator, the late Estes Kefauver, of Tennessee, had moved into a spot that would soon enable him to take on the price study Magnuson had been asking for—and a lot more. In January, 1957, Kefauver had taken over as the new chairman of the Senate Subcommittee on Antitrust and Monopoly. Although he had attained this position through the usual seniority system, he had unusual qualifications for the job. After graduating from the Yale Law School in 1927, he went into private practice in Chattanooga, and, as he recalled in the fall of 1961, two years before he died, "Even in those days I had an interest in monopoly problems in general. My mother's double first cousin, Uncle Patrick Estes, was general counsel and part owner of the Life & Casualty Insurance Co. of Tennessee, and I was very close to him. Although he was a lawyer for big business, he was deeply worried about the number of small businesses that were going under. He felt that the important economic decisions were made in the cities and that the little fellows who were affected across the country couldn't do much of anything about it. I became convinced that the only possible way to change the trend was to increase competition. To do that, we have to apply the antitrust laws that we have more vigorously, and if they're not enough, we have to revise them. I believe that a man who is elected by the people to serve in Congress ought to pick out something that is in the public interest and specialize in it, whether or not it's popular, so when I took my seat in the House, in 1939, I made antitrust matters my specialty. As a result, I was put on the Committee on the Judiciary and the Committee on Small Business, in both of which we studied economic concentration. Naturally I became interested in increasing government procurement from small businesses. Then I got busy trying to plug a loophole in Section Seven of the Clayton Antitrust Act in order to further discourage monopoly by forbidding one company to gain control of another by buying up its assets. We finally got that passed, in the Celler-Kefauver bill, in 1950, the year after I got to the Senate. It was through the courts' interpretation of Congress's intent in that bill that du Pont was recently forced to get rid of its General Motors stock. Still, that was a limited success. I keep feeling that mergers, consolidations, and coöperation between large blocs of economic power are on the increase, and that this is bound to lead to total abuse of our free-enterprise system, and, inevitably, to total state control —in short, statism. And that is something none of us want. Some of the more responsible corporate managers I've talked with are concerned about this, too. But a lot of others don't even realize the danger, or if they do, they don't care."

Kefauver's efforts to curb the concentration of economic power brought him little public notice, but in 1950 he struck at a different kind of power—organized crime—and overnight became a national figure. In 1951, the Washington press corps voted him the second-best senator (Paul Douglas, of Illinois, was first), but at the same time many observers were calling him a mere publicity hunter. "Here in Washington, the cynical explanation for his success is his great buildup as a crimebuster on the nation's television screens," wrote

Marquis Child in 1952. "But the real reason may be the sheer novelty of a man who is saying something out of his mind and out of his heart about the basic issue of power and its use and abuse in mid-century America." While the crime investigation made Kefauver a potential nominee for the Presidency, it also ruined his chances. By revealing that his party occasionally had ties with the underworld, especially in the large cities, he forfeited the support of some key political bosses and, ultimately, of the party leadership.

In any case, Kefauver was never really an influential member of the Senate. When it came time for the Democratic leadership to line up blocs of votes, no one approached him, for, as a man not given to the usual logrolling, he could seldom command any vote except his own. In 1954, when he was up for reëlection, he took three politically hazardous positions. He was one of the initiators of the petition to censure Senator Joseph R. McCarthy. He refused to sign the Southern Manifesto against civil rights for Negroes. (Southern conservatives had always disliked him for his liberalism; now they had cause to hate him, and most of them did.) And he cast a lone vote during debate on a bill outlawing the Communist Party, when the Democrats, to show that they weren't soft on Communism, submitted an amendment that would have made membership in the Party punishable as a crime; the vote was eighty-one for and Kefauver against. When he got back to his office, one of his assistants said that all hope for the election was lost, and burst into tears. Kefauver patted the man on the back. "It had to be done," he said. "The bill is unconstitutional." Later, President Eisenhower said much the same thing about the amendment, and then J. Edgar Hoover pointed out that it would make his job more difficult, whereupon Congress dropped the matter.

"Estes has more guts than anyone I've ever known," a highly placed Democratic senator said later. "I can't say that I agree with him on every issue, but whenever I find myself on the other side, I always feel a little uneasy."

One reason that Kefauver was not warmly regarded by some of his colleagues in the Senate was that he did not always carry his share of the load on committees headed by somebody else, and they saw this tendency as another sign that he was interested less in doing the tedious work that is the everyday lot of a senator than in seeking the limelight. Another was that, even to his closest friends and political associates, he was an enigma. His coonskin campaigning cap notwithstanding, Kefauver was essentially an intellectual (in 1948 the American Political Science Association made him its first non-academic officer), and he was also deeply introverted and taciturn. "I've never known a man who played his cards so close to the vest," one senator who worked closely with him in many struggles for progressive legislation has said. "You never knew what he was going to do next—and half the time, after he'd done it, you didn't know why." Often, when word got around that Kefauver was about to take an issue to the floor of the Senate, the younger liberals gathered in the rear of the chamber to watch him in action, both because he was a political maneuverer worth studying and because they were endlessly curious about how a man who had fought for the principles they believed in had survived politically for nearly a quarter of a century. A large man—standing six feet three inches tall and weighing two hundred and twenty pounds—Kefauver ordinarily sat stolidly at his desk near the front of the chamber, his large hands in his lap and his narrow, ruddy face totally without expression. When he rose to speak, he was seldom impressive; unshakably polite, he mumbled almost inaudibly, he hesitated for long stretches, and he invariably threw away his best lines. Even so, he was rarely underestimated by anyone more than once. "Kefauver gets up with that slow drawl of his, talking so softly you can hardly hear him," remarked a Republican opponent after a bitter debate. "You lean forward to catch his words, and you discover he's beating your brains out."

III

When Kefauver began looking around for a staff for the Subcommittee on Antitrust and Monopoly, it did not take him long to choose his two principal assistants; Paul Rand Dixon, an F.T.C. lawyer from Tennessee with a reputation for vigorous trustbusting, became his staff director and chief counsel, and Blair became his chief economist. The Senator and Blair had known each other since 1945, when Blair, then an economist with the government's Smaller War Plants Corporation, had testified before the House Small Business Committee. When the session broke up, Kefauver had asked Blair to have lunch with him and talk over some of the problems facing small business, and after that lunch the association between the two men had deepened. From time to time, Kefauver had called on Blair to do some economic spadework in the antitrust field, and over the years had come to rely on him more and more. Each man considered himself a hard-bitten realist and looked with both admiration and a sort of fond condescension on the other's struggles to create a more equitable world. Senator Paul Douglas, in his book *Ethics in Government,* mentions Blair as the exemplary civil servant, and

Kefauver clearly agreed. "John is an idealist, but he's an extremely able, hard-working man, and his facts are always accurate to the last decimal point," he once said. As for Blair, he viewed Senator Kefauver as a man of great intellectual capacity and also as the last of the Populists—a rural individualist battling vast urban economic interests at all but hopeless odds. "Estes fought for the public interest with remarkable restraint and fairness," he told an acquaintance a few days after Kefauver's death. "And he showed great courage, when you consider that he struck at the heart of where the power lies."

Up to the time that Kefauver took over the Subcommittee on Antitrust and Monopoly, its splashiest venture had been the investigation of the Dixon-Yates contract, in 1955, which had been conducted by a three-senator panel under Kefauver's supervision. When he took the chair, he had to decide what the subcommittee should investigate next, and Blair had the answer. For a dozen years, he had spent a good deal of his spare time studying what some economists call "administered prices"—a concept originally formulated in 1935 by Gardiner Means, a New Deal economist, who used the term to describe prices that, instead of being dictated by the competition of the market place, were "set by administrative action and held constant for a period of time." Prices are administered, Means held, when the demand for a commodity has fallen off and management cuts back on production and keeps prices up. According to Means, the use of administered prices was particularly revealing in certain special circumstances—when leading producers sell at the same price despite differences in their costs and profits, for instance, and when the big fellows in a field adopt the prices set by the biggest fellow.

Although Means's theory had been widely accepted for some years, it had gradually fallen into disuse by economists, primarily those in academic circles, who felt that its earlier promise had not been supported by the facts. Blair, however, had become increasingly convinced of its value as an interpretive tool, and was determined to revive the idea. "It seemed to me that the behavior of administered prices was a highly appropriate subject for the subcommittee to look into," Blair has said. "Under our present antitrust laws, there's no effective way to handle administered-price abuses, unless the Department of Justice and the F.T.C. can produce concrete evidence of collusion to fix prices, and that is precisely the thing that is most difficult to produce."

Kefauver agreed with Blair that the subject was a good one, and over the next two years the subcommittee investigated and held hearings on two basic industries—steel and automobiles—in which, as Kefauver later reported to the subcommittee's parent body, the Committee on the Judiciary, "there exists a kind of upside-down competition where prices continue to go up even when production remains low or declines." He went on, "These high prices were put into effect by the respective leaders in these industries, with the other members following with identical prices. Higher prices resulting from such a pricing system are unchecked by either privately initiated competition or application of antitrust laws. This is the crux of the problem."

Gradually, the vast compilation of data that Blair and his staff collected on the subject of administered prices began to convince more and more economists—in academic circles and out—that the theory was, indeed, a useful one. Today, it has been put back in some economics textbooks, and, in fact, the term even appears from time to time in newspapers and magazines without the quotation marks that always bracketed it before the subcommittee began looking into the subject.

Late in 1957, between the steel hearings and the automobile hearings, Blair prevailed upon Dr. Till to join his staff, and one day he asked her advice on what they should look into next. Without hesitation, she answered, "Drugs." The suggestion interested Blair—because of their experience at the F.T.C. and because he himself had become chary not only of the cost of new drugs but of something else—their side effects. His wife's brother, Wesley Finney, and his wife, Elizabeth, were both severely crippled by rheumatoid arthritis. "When cortisone was first tested, back around 1950, there was a tremendous publicity barrage to the effect that suffering from arthritis was now a thing of the past," Blair has recalled. "I remember that one magazine had a cover picture of a man jumping with glee, and the story inside told of his having been a bedridden cripple before using the drug. Elizabeth and Wesley saw that article, and begged their doctor for cortisone. He prescribed it. It gave them more freedom of movement and decreased their pain, but it later had fearful side effects that nobody had warned them about—peptic ulcers and moonface, where your head swells up like a basketball. That was one thing, and then I found out that Elizabeth and Wesley were paying between sixty and seventy dollars a month for cortisone alone."

In the end, though, Blair felt compelled to reject Dr. Till's suggestion—temporarily, at any rate. "There were plenty of good reasons for not going into it," he said later. "First of all, it was a hideously complex business, and there was nothing in the way of reference works on it, because the drug industry had never been adequately studied by anybody, officially or privately. Then, there was a totally new and abstruse nomenclature. And, finally, no basic figures on production costs were available. Naturally, if you're going to have any kind of thorough price investigation, you must have those."

In the fall of 1958, when the automobile hearings came to an end, Blair again asked Dr. Till what she thought the subcommittee should look into next, and again he got the answer "Drugs." This time, there was a bit more to go on, for the previous February Congressman John A. Blatnik, of Minnesota, chairman of the Legal and Monetary Affairs Subcommittee of the House Committee on Government Operations, had held hearings to determine whether the F.T.C. had been doing a proper job of policing the advertising of tranquillizers. The hearings were inconclusive, however: they lasted only four days; no one, it seemed, could decide exactly what sort of jurisdiction the F.T.C. had over this field; and the majority of the witnesses were inclined to defend the drug industry down the line. A few were highly critical, though—among them Dr. J. Murray Steele, professor of medicine at New York University and chairman of the New York Academy of Medicine's Committee on Public Health, who registered a strong complaint about "the extravagant and distorted literature which some of the drug houses are distributing to the medical profession." This material was misleading in two respects, he declared. "First, it may recommend a product in such a way as to lead to, if not encourage, its indiscriminate use," he said. "Secondly, some manufacturers' literature . . . contains . . . little or no mention of side effects and contra-indications to the use of tranquillizers." Dr. Ian Stevenson, chairman of the Department of Neurology and Psychiatry at the University of Virginia, was somewhat more specific. "I might mention Drug A, which was marketed across the country after only two clinical studies had been published, containing negligible mention of side effects," he testified. "Subsequently, harmful side effects of this drug were published—I know four references—and yet subsequent advertising of this drug has continued to neglect and minimize side effects."

This was as specific as he was permitted to be, for the lead-off witness, Dr. Nathan S. Kline, director of research at Rockland State Hospital, in New York, had prevailed upon the subcommittee not to let any drugs or their manufacturers be mentioned by name; it would be "very much against the public interest," he said. In Kefauver's view, this decision was a serious mistake. "If doctors and, ultimately, their patients are being misled in matters of such importance, it should be made known," he explained later. "Without arousing the public, you can't hope to correct such a situation."

Besides the transcript of the Blatnik hearings, Drs. Blair and Till had the long-delayed F.T.C. antibiotics study, which had finally been published in the summer of 1958, after Magnuson had said at the appropriations hearings that year, "I wrote the Commission, I think, three or four times in the past three or four months, regarding this, because I, as well as many senators, have received a tremendous amount of mail on the high price of drugs." As it turned out, though, the report contained little that was suited to the staff's purposes. While it provided some promising leads, a helpful appendix, and a profusion of charts and graphs, there was nothing on basic production costs. Once more, Blair rejected the idea of investigating the drug business, choosing instead to examine certain areas of the bread industry.

Then, one rainy afternoon a few weeks later, Blair happened to be glancing through the F.T.C.'s latest quarterly financial report—a statistical résumé of the income, liabilities, invested capital, and profits of all manufacturing corporations, broken down into about two dozen industries, from "Aircraft and Parts" to "Tobacco Manufacturers." In the previous quarterly reports he had looked at, the drug industry had been lumped in with the chemical industry, but this one listed it separately, and Blair was amazed to find that its profit came to 18.9 per cent of invested capital after taxes, and 10.8 per cent of sales after taxes. The figures were considerably higher than those for any of the other industries. In fact, they were more than twice the average of all the manufacturing concerns included in the report.

Blair telephoned Dr. Till, and she hurried over to his office. "My God, just look at those profits!" he said, waving the report at her.

She was as surprised as he had been. "I'd never seen anything like it," she said later. "It was unheard of for a whole industry to have profits like that. The more successful pharmaceutical houses were obviously having a fantastic windfall. Nothing as wild as those figures had ever occurred to me. John said to get on it, so I dropped the bread business and went to work on drugs that very day."

Soon the staff had still more to go on—the results of a private investigation by John Lear, the science editor of the *Saturday Review*. In the summer of 1958, a woman reader had written to him, asking for information on the proper use of various antibiotics. Lear answered that he wasn't a physician, and suggested that she consult her family doctor. A few days later, he got another letter from her, in which she said that she *had* consulted her doctor, that he, too, was confused about antibiotics, and that he thought it would be a public service to have the subject clarified by responsible authorities. Lear then approached several medical-research experts at leading universities, and he learned from them that many doctors were confused about new drugs, including antibiotics.

In the first place, they told him, there were by this time dozens of such drugs on the market, many no more than slight modifications of earlier ones, some combining antibiotics with antihistamines, hormones, or vitamins, and almost all developed as a result of frenzied competition in the pharmaceutical industry. Lear was also told that, with regard to drugs generally, a number of the new products were not improvements over the old ones. Some were actually less efficacious, and some had little efficacy at all. Beyond that, drugs were often put on the market before the results of clinical tests on them were published, and as much as six months before the American Medical Association's Council on Drugs got around to appraising them, so it was frequently impossible for even a specialist to find out what a given drug might do for a patient. As an example, doctors had been prescribing antibiotics for everything from a mild cold (for which they were useless) to a minor infection (for which they were unnecessary), and this random approach had produced resistant strains of bacteria, like the invigorated staphylococcus that caused some five hundred epidemics in hospitals across the country between 1954 and 1958.

One evening, Lear had dinner with an eminent research physician, and afterward the two men visited a laboratory in the hospital where the doctor worked. "He pulled open several drawers that were full of drug samples and advertisements," Lear said later. " 'Just take a look at that stuff!' he told me, and then went on to say that a good part of the advertising was misleading—in fact, that some of it was downright fraudulent. Finally, he said, 'Look, you're walking around a big story. Why don't you step into it?' I said I might if I had enough information. Among other things, he showed me a small folder advertising Sigmamycin, an antibiotic put out by Chas. Pfizer, Inc. Across the top of the folder was a banner of bold type that said, 'Every day, everywhere, more and more physicians find Sigmamycin the antibiotic therapy of choice.' Below that were reproductions of what appeared to be the professional cards of eight doctors around the country, with addresses, telephone numbers, and office hours. The doctor said he had himself conducted some experiments with Sigmamycin, and at one point he had written to the eight doctors to ask the outcome of their use of the drug in clinical tests. As he told me this, he reached into one of the drawers and brought out eight envelopes, all stamped 'Return to Writer—Unclaimed.' I asked him if I might report his experience, and he said that he couldn't get involved in any kind of exposé. He pointed out, however, that there was nothing to prevent me from writing to the doctors myself." Lear did write to them, and all eight letters came back. Then he sent telegrams to the doctors, and was informed that there were no such addresses. Finally, he attempted to telephone them, and learned that there were no such telephone numbers. Lear thereupon wrote an article entitled "Taking the Miracle Out of the Miracle Drugs," dealing with the general misuse of antibiotics and describing the incident of the professional cards. The piece appeared in the *Saturday Review* for January 3, 1959, and Kefauver later said that it helped, as much as anything else, to spur on the investigation and to broaden its range.

IV

Some time before that, word had got out about the subcommittee's interest in the pharmaceutical business. On November 17, 1958, a headline in the *Oil, Paint & Drug Reporter,* a weekly trade journal, announced "Kefauver Prepares to Scatter Buckshot at the Drug Industry." Apparently the industry took the news in its stride, for a month later the same periodical noted, "Drug Outlook for 1959 Seen Wonderful." In January, Kefauver called a meeting of the subcommittee—then consisting of Democratic Senators Joseph C. O'Mahoney, Thomas C. Hennings, Jr., John A. Carroll, and Philip A. Hart, and Republican Senators William Langer, Everett McKinley Dirksen, and Alexander Wiley—and proposed a general, tentative examination of a number of enterprises that seemed to be using administered prices, including the bread industry, manufacturers of paper boxes and of replacement parts for farm machinery, the fertilizer industry, automobile-financing companies, and the producers of rubber tires, aluminum, and drugs. The entire package was approved without dissent. However, in view of the paucity of the evidence obtained thus far, it was by no means assured that any of the investigations would result in public hearings.

A few days later, Dr. Till made her first contribution to what was to become a huge compilation of data—a report called "Pharmaceuticals," which described some of the byways that the staff could profitably follow, and paused here and there to fill in portions of the landscape. To begin with, she observed that in 1957 pharmaceutical sales at the wholesale level were estimated to have run to two and a quarter billion dollars, of which ethical, or prescription, drugs accounted for three-quarters. Of the ethicals—the staff's sole concern from the start—the biggest sellers were the antibiotics. From Dr. Till's report and from work subsequently done by other members of the subcommittee staff, Kefauver learned not just about antibiotics but about the drug industry's general method of operation. In looking into the development of the antibiotics, the staff started at the beginning—with Sir Alexander Fleming's discovery of penicillin, in 1929. Fleming realized that penicillin had a potent, if obscure, effect on certain bacteria, but it wasn't until 1941 that other British researchers proved that the drug was highly efficacious in treating septic wounds. That year, the United States government became eager to determine whether it could be produced in quantity, and two British researchers were brought to this country, under the auspices of the Office of Scientific Research and Development, to try to get private pharmaceutical houses interested in working on the project. They had almost no luck. A few weeks after the attack on Pearl Harbor, Dr. Vannevar Bush, director of the O.S.R.D., personally brought a number of drug firms into the picture. Almost a year and a half later, in the spring of 1943, they had accomplished little in the way of quantity production, and on April 27th Dr. Bush wrote a letter to Elihu Root, Jr., then a consultant to the Army Air Forces: "Now, the pharmaceutical companies have coöperated in this affair after a fashion. They have not made their experimental results and their development of manufacturing processes generally available, however. . . . This is the problem. It obviously needs some very careful handling." As it turned out, the problem was that most firms were too busy trying to corner patents on various processes in the production of penicillin to produce much of it, and the government began pressing them to work together. It was slow going. On January 19, 1944, Dr. Albert L. Elder, the coördinator of a special penicillin program run by the War Production Board, sent a memorandum to Fred J. Stock, head of the Drugs and Cosmetics Section of the W.P.B., complaining about the refusal of the drug firms to exchange information, and added, "The value of penicillin in saving the lives of wounded soldiers has been so thoroughly demonstrated that I cannot with a clear conscience assume the responsibility for coördinating this program any longer while at the same time being handicapped by being unable to make available information which would result in the output of more penicillin and thereby save the lives of our soldiers."

By then, an obscure outpost of a government agency was far ahead of the drug firms; the scientists of a Department of Agriculture laboratory in Peoria, Illinois, were rapidly evolving a method of large-scale production. Soon, the department filed its own patent applications, and they were granted, whereupon, under its regulations, all of its patents were made available to any producer without charge. By the time the war ended, the production of penicillin had reached some seven billion units—an average shot may be six hundred thousand units—and the drug had saved the lives of thousands of servicemen. After the war, more and more drug firms began making and selling the drug in a stiffly competitive race; within eight years the price had fallen from two hundred dollars per million units to sixty cents per million units.

Since penicillin had been produced from a common mold, the drug companies concluded that other antibiotics, with perhaps even greater therapeutic powers, might be produced from other molds. The firms had the necessary equipment for such production left over from their war work, and they had the necessary scientists, too, so they went to work, and in a short time they came up with a dazzling array of new drugs. In 1945, Rutgers, under a grant from Merck, discovered streptomycin. In 1947, Yale, under a grant from Parke, Davis, discovered chloramphenicol. In 1948, Lederle discovered chlortetracycline. And in 1949, Chas. Pfizer discovered oxytetracycline. (Like the name penicillin, these are all generic names—that is, names that are supposed to provide a clue to the chemical composition of the drugs. A given drug also has a precise chemical name, and it may be sold under one or more trade names.)

The going price of each of these six drugs, the staff learned, was inversely related to competition in its sales. Penicillin, of course, was the cheapest of the lot. Streptomycin was patented, but it had been licensed to several companies to produce it on a royalty-payment basis. As a result, it was relatively competitive, and could be purchased for less than ten cents a shot. By contrast, chloramphenicol, chlortetracycline, and oxytetracycline—known as broad-spectrum antibiotics, because they were highly effective against a far wider range of harmful bacteria than the others —promised not only a kind of revolution in medical care but a bonanza in profits. They were produced and sold exclusively by their patentees and solely under trade names—Chloromycetin, Aureomycin, and Terramycin, respectively

—and each of them still sold for the fifty cents a pill that Hamilton had paid eight years before. Since the manufacturers of penicillin were presumably making a profit, Kefauver and his staff concluded that Pfizer, Lederle, and Parke, Davis—using similar facilities, and with higher yields from improved production methods—must have been reaping a rich harvest indeed.

Another thing Blair and his co-workers looked into was the relations among the big companies. All the available information, the Till report observed, indicated "a fraternity of spirit among the large manufacturers," resulting from their attempts to preserve the foundation of their prosperity, the patent system, by means of which they were able to control the market for the most profitable drugs. Noting that "companies . . . avoid litigation of patents," the report went on to say that they apparently preferred to settle "by private agreement . . . who should file and secure the patent" when there was any contention over who had been first, and, subsequently, to decide among themselves who would be licensed to produce or sell the drug under royalty agreements.

As Kefauver saw it, the drug companies' unwillingness to test the validity of their patent claims in court probably meant that they felt the whole patent setup in the drug field to be rather shaky. "The Patent Office had traditionally ruled that products of nature were not patentable," he explained later. "It refused to grant a patent for cortisone on the ground that it was a product of nature. Streptomycin was developed from a natural mold, but the argument was put forward that the substance was a transitory product of nature that had never been isolated before and that its therapeutic use had been unknown. The Patent Office went along with this—why, I'll never understand—so all the later antibiotics became patentable, too."

Dr. Till's report also asserted that there was "a close identity of prices" in the drug industry; that the industry followed the practice of "price leadership," with the big firms doing the leading; that there was little foreign competition; that newcomers' entrance into the market was all but impossible; and that there had been "a merger trend in recent years."

V Between 1958 and 1961, members of the subcommittee talked with more than three hundred people, of whom John Lear was one of the first. Shortly after his article appeared, Drs. Blair and Till visited him at his office in New York, and he gave them a number of helpful tips, many of which had come to him in the mail in response to the article. As it turned out, the most valuable leads that he had at the time were the names of medical specialists, including both research men and professors in medical schools, along with a few men who were, or had been, employed as consultants by drug companies. These people outlined for Drs. Blair and Till the development, the use, the efficacy, and the dangers of various drugs that had appeared in the past dozen years, and referred them to books and medical journals for further details. Once the two had learned the basic terminology from the doctors they talked with, they could understand most of the articles written for the general practitioner.

At this stage, the subcommittee staff consisted of thirty-eight people, including lawyers, researchers, secretaries, clerks, and some part-time employees. Because most of them were busy preparing for the hearings on the bread industry and other matters, the drug investigation was left almost entirely to a group of eight: Dr. Blair; Dr. Till; Mrs. Lucile Burd Wendt, who had worked on the 1958 F.T.C. antibiotics study, and who, as a bacteriologist, chemist, and lawyer on loan from the Patent Office, where she had been a patent examiner for biochemical products and processes, was a triple-threat member of the team; Dr. E. Wayles Browne, a statistical economist, who, having been brought up as a Christian Scientist, had had no personal experience with drugs but whose expertise in reducing complex statistics to understandable charts and graphs was unmatched; Dr. Walter S. Measday, a professor of economics at the University of Maryland, who assisted on a part-time basis; two attorneys, Mrs. Dorothy Goodwin and George E. Clifford, who did much of the investigative legwork; and Mrs. Emily Zayyani, a staff secretary, who not only collated the research material that the others had collected but contributed a good bit herself.

Among the reports that the group produced was one on hormone drugs, which ranked close to antibiotics in volume of sales. Written by Dr. Till and completed in mid-February of 1959, it concentrated on what was to become the first field of battle between the subcommittee and the industry—the cortisone derivatives, most commonly known as the cortical steroids and less commonly known as the corticosteroids, the corticoids, the adrenal steroids, the adrenocorticotrophic hormones, the steroid hormones, and the steroids. Cortisone was first isolated from extracts of the adrenal cortex in 1936 by E. C. Kendall, at the Mayo Clinic. Researchers were certain that the extract would have potent effects on the bodily mechanism, but not enough of it could be obtained by Kendall's method to make clinical tests. Then, eight years later, Dr. L. H. Sarett, working on the same problem at the Merck laboratory, discovered a way to synthesize cortisone from ox bile and produced enough of it to perform tests, and, in 1948, an initial series were made at the clinic by Dr. Philip S. Hench. He presently discovered that the hormone appeared to have a radically beneficial effect in a wide variety of pathological states—among them, rheumatoid arthritis, intractable asthma, lupus erythematosis, gout, Addison's disease, Hodgkin's disease, lymphatic leukemia, rheumatic fever, and tetanus.

The prospects for commercial production of cortisone were bleak, though, for it took Merck thirty-seven complex chemical steps, occupying several months, to produce a small batch of it. In 1950, according to Dr. Floyd S. Daft, director of the National Institute of Arthritis and Metabolic Diseases, "it was estimated that the production of enough cortisone to treat one patient for one year would require the slaughter of 14,600 head of cattle." The cost of an ounce of cortisone, he added, was forty-eight hundred dollars, or more than a hundred times the price of gold. Over the next couple of years, Merck managed to cut the number of chemical steps to twenty and to increase substantially the yield of cortisone per pound of ox bile. The cost went down. Then, in 1952, the Upjohn Company devised a method of producing cortisone by fermentation from Mexican yams, which were considerably more plentiful than ox bile. In effect, the steps were reduced again, and the cost dropped further. But the price of the drug, according to Dr. Till's findings, did not drop to a level that reflected the great savings in production costs.

No sooner had cortisone come into wider use than three important new facts were learned about it. First, it was by no means a cure, for its effects lasted only as long as the drug was administered. Second, it was hazardously congenial to such micro-organisms as streptococci, staphylococci, typhoid bacilli, spirochetes, and the viruses of poliomyelitis and influenza. Third, and most important of all, it produced such acute side effects as softening of the bones, gross obesity, facial hair in women and children, severe acne, hypertension, peptic ulcers, diabetes, and psychosis.

Early in 1955, the Schering Corporation put on the market two new cortical steroids, generically named prednisone and prednisolone, which it sold under the trade names Meticorten and Meticortelone. "With these products, Schering hit the jackpot," Dr. Till noted. Although they were similar to cortisone, they were four to five times as potent and appeared to have fewer side effects. The Patent Office decided that prednisone and prednisolone were sufficient improvements on nature to be patentable, and in this case the big companies did not come to an agreement. Not only Schering but four other firms—Upjohn, Merck, Pfizer, and Parke, Davis—applied for patents, causing the Office to declare that what is called a patent interference existed. This meant that until the conflict could be resolved by the Patent Office, none of the companies had a monopoly on the two drugs, and all could sell them at will. The stakes were considerable. "In 1957, sixty-five million dollars' worth of these two drugs were sold," Dr. Till asserted. Since none of the companies were willing to give up their claims, the contest went on—and it is still going on.

But the conflict by no means meant that the five companies involved were not on speaking terms. On the con-

trary, according to subpoenaed documents subsequently made public by the subcommittee, they agreed that whichever of them won the patent would license the others to sell the drugs on a royalty basis; that in the meantime, for three years, the four other companies would pay Schering a three-per-cent royalty; and that none of them would let anyone who was not a party to the agreement buy either drug in bulk form (that is, as finished powder that had only to be tableted and packaged).

Later, defending the agreement, Senator Dirksen declared, "It is a disservice to challenge an agreement which makes a new development available to the public and improves our general standard of health even though it may add a relatively small amount to the benefits of the company that believes it is responsible for the development in question."

Kefauver agreed that the five companies wanted to get the drug on the market as soon as possible—but not solely for the benefit of the public. "The Schering licensing agreement on prednisone is of particular interest," he said, "because on the basis of patent applications, it establishes marketing restrictions designed to prevent small companies from marketing this drug."

To the dismay of the five companies, a small drug company did put prednisone on the market. Soon after the agreement was reached, Syntex, a Mexican firm with a top-notch research laboratory, began selling the drug in this country in bulk form. Schering slapped an infringement-of-patent-rights suit on Syntex, which turned right around and slapped one on Schering, stating that it had actually discovered prednisone first—a claim that was later supported by the Pharmaceutical Manufacturers Association, the

N.A.M. of the drug business. When Syntex put bulk prednisone on the market, the smaller drug companies bought what they could get of it and began selling it widely—and far more cheaply than their larger competitors did. Before long, Merck and Pfizer decided to enter the race, and started selling both prednisone and prednisolone to small companies in bulk form. The result was that while Schering, Merck, Pfizer, Upjohn, and Parke, Davis were selling the two drugs, under their trade names, to pharmacists at the uniform price of $17.90 per hundred five-milligram tablets, the smaller companies were asking as little as a quarter of that amount for the same quantity of either of them under their generic names.

VI

After Dr. Till had submitted her report, she and Blair began dropping in on druggists to check on the quantities of generically named drugs that were being bought by the public. They were puzzled to learn that it was rare for a druggist to receive a prescription for a drug under its generic name. Next, they compiled a list of small pharmaceutical firms that produced drugs and sold them on a generic-name basis, and visited some of their plants to get an idea of their operations. The first thing they found out was that while few individual consumers bought drugs under their generic names, a good many hospitals, clinics, and local, state, and federal agencies did. Then, after weeding out any drug companies that the Food and Drug Administration had cracked down on for putting out impure products, Blair selected a few firms—small, medium, and large—and asked Browne to plot their wholesale prices on a chart. It was clear at a glance that the larger a company was, the higher its prices were set, and the more likely it was to sell its goods under trade names.

Now even more puzzled by the failure of most doctors to prescribe low-priced generic drugs, Blair and other members of the staff spent some of their off hours questioning physicians about this. To a man, they explained that they didn't have the time to look into the reputations of the various small concerns and chose to play it safe. Also, several of them pointed out that most detail men (pharmaceuticalese for salesmen who call on doctors) hinted darkly at the substandard quality of drugs put out by small companies. Moreover, when a physician sat down to write out a prescription, he found it far simpler to remember, say, Sterane, Pfizer's trade name for prednisone, than the name prednisone itself. (Practically speaking, drug companies were free to give their drugs any generic names they liked, and many of them, according to some experts, had a way of choosing an awkward generic name so that the trade name would be the one to stick in the doctor's mind.) The physicians explained, further, that large pharmaceutical houses subjected them to a barrage of advertising and promotional material in which generic names were scarcely mentioned, and that detail men visited them almost daily.

"The principal function of a detail man is to persuade physicians to use the trademarked drugs put out by his particular house," Blair said after the investigation was completed. "Some of the smaller manufacturers told us that they couldn't support a staff of detail men, but Upjohn, for instance, with fifty-seven hundred employees, had more than a thousand detail men. I daresay that no sizable firm in any other industry has one salesman for every five workers."

By the winter of 1959, Kefauver, like Magnuson and other senators, had received some letters from consumers about the prices of drugs. While many were crank complaints of the sort that reach every senator's desk every day, others were sensible and informative, among them one from an American lawyer who was in London on business. Being a diabetic, he had taken along a large supply of Orinase, Upjohn's brand of tolbutamide—a new oral antidiabetic drug, which many patients could use in place of insulin. But his work had kept him abroad longer than he had anticipated, and he ran out of medicine, whereupon a doctor in London gave him a prescription for the same drug, which is sold in Britain under the trade name Rastinon. Rastinon, the lawyer wrote, was less than half as expensive in England as Orinase was in this country. Kefauver and Blair discussed means of getting information on the foreign prices of other drugs. Blair confessed that he could see no simple way of accomplishing this, but Kefauver soon came up with a solution—he simply wrote to the State Department and asked it to have our consulates abroad check. Before long, the information began coming in. Percentages varied, but in most cases the prices were lower abroad.

Next, Kefauver suggested that the staff find out what prices pharmaceutical concerns charged non-profit agencies for certain drugs. Clifford was given this job, and he went first to the Military Medical Supply Agency, which serves as the central purchasing arm of all dispensaries and hospitals run by the armed forces, and also purchases medical supplies, on request, for the Public Health Service, the Office of Civil and Defense Mobilization, and our military-assistance program. M.M.S.A. naturally buys as cheaply as it can, provided its standards of quality are maintained, and it sees to it that they are. In response to some of Clifford's questions, the executive director of M.M.S.A., Rear Admiral William L. Knickerbocker, told him that bids on patented drugs, including antibiotics, were uniformly high. On the subject of cortical steroids, however, Clifford learned that on February 3, 1959, M.M.S.A. had advertised that it wanted to buy 1,056,000 tablets of prednisone in thousand-tablet bottles. Six days later, the contract was awarded to the Premo Pharmaceutical Laboratories, a small New Jersey firm, at a price of $20.98 per bottle. Two other small companies had submitted bids that were roughly a dollar and two dollars per bottle higher, and the fourth-lowest bidder was none other than the Schering Corporation, which asked $23.63 a bottle.

"When I saw that in Clifford's report, I realized that we had our first big breakthrough," Blair recalled later. "We knew that Premo sold prednisone to the commercial trade for around thirty-one dollars, or roughly fifty per cent more than its bid to M.M.S.A. Naturally, it could cut its price substantially for a government contract, because of the size of the order. However, Schering sold its prednisone to the trade for a hundred and seventy dollars per bottle, or six hundred and twenty per cent above its quotation to M.M.S.A. Obviously, it counted on making a profit when it tendered its bid to the government, so we could only conclude that its profit on commercial transactions must be fantastic."

Kefauver was impressed when Blair showed him what the staff had found, and was even more impressed when Browne compiled some profit figures for his edification. Using financial publications like *Moody's Industrial Manual* and the *Fortune Directory*, Browne discovered that when it came

to profits as a percentage of invested capital after taxes, thirteen drug companies were among the top fifty companies in America, and three drug companies—Carter Products, American Home Products, and Smith, Kline & French—led the field—with net profits of 38.2 per cent, 33.5 per cent, and 33.1 per cent, respectively.

"That meant, for instance, that Carter's net profit before federal corporation taxes of fifty-two per cent was about seventy-five per cent—an unheard-of-figure," Blair said after these statistics had been made public. "I couldn't believe Browne's figures. Just to make sure, I asked the F.T.C. to prepare similar compilations. They did, and their figures were slightly higher than ours. So we took them to Estes. He didn't believe them, either. He asked if we had checked them with the F.T.C., and when I said we had, he told me to double-check those that were over thirty per cent. So we did, and the F.T.C. double-checked, too. The two of us got the same results."

The Senator still found the whole thing difficult to believe. "I thought that profits like those were excessive by any test you put them to—particularly in a field where every effort should be made to get prices down," he later explained. "Such profits meant that Carter, American Home Products, and Smith, Kline & French could pay off their capital investment in two or three years."

Although Kefauver and his staff felt that they were on to something that called for further study, they were still faced with the problem of finding out how much it cost the companies to produce their drugs. At the time, Blair wrote a memorandum to Dixon, saying, "In theory the best method of determining the reasonableness of a price is to compare it with costs. In practice, however, cost information is usually difficult to obtain. . . . The drug industry is already exhibiting to the Federal Trade Commission strenuous opposition to the divulgence of cost information, threatening to take the issue to the Supreme Court." But if the hearings were to be fully effective, cost data had to be obtained one way or another. "Without such figures, we knew that we'd be pilloried," Blair later explained. "The drug people could merely say that their prices were high because their costs were high, and who could gainsay them? We were faced with the fact that many firms don't keep costs for individual products, and those that do usually allocate the indirect, or overhead, costs by some arbitrary formula. Anyway, we met week after week to consider this problem of costs, and got absolutely nowhere. How necessary it was to get the figures we wanted, and how hopeless it seemed!"

A month or so after Browne came up with his profit figures, he happened to notice in a 1957 report by the Tariff Commission called "Synthetic Organic Chemicals—United States Production and Sales" a list of which companies produced which drugs. He was surprised to find that often only one or two companies produced a given drug, and was more surprised to find, by checking against industry trade lists, that many other companies sold the same drug. "This is unique in American industry," Blair said later. "One of the more extreme cases was Parke, Davis, which sold twenty of fifty-one major drug products included in our study, but produced only one, Chloromycetin. We figured that the extraordinary interlocking relationships of the large drug companies might produce something of interest, and decided to look into it further. Finally, we found the answer. Before the war, there were two kinds of drug concerns—chemical firms, which manufactured bulk powder, and drug houses, which processed the powder and sold it in finished form. When the wonder drugs came along, the bulk-chemical firms became aware of the enormous profits to be made on them in the retail market, so they went into it, although they continued to manufacture certain items and sell them in bulk to other companies. Then, it dawned on us—of course, the big companies were now buying from and selling to each other. That meant that they had patent-licensing agreements and purchase-and-sale contracts that would show just how pally an arrangement it all was. We didn't know exactly how to go about getting these, so we took what we had to Estes. He went over it carefully, and then said, 'Why, let's get out some subpoenas.'"

On March 26, 1959, subpoenas went out to nineteen major drug companies, ordering them to submit their patent-licensing agreements and purchase-and-sale contracts on a wide variety of drugs. Since there was little to do until the subpoenaed documents came in, Blair made a trip to St. Petersburg, Florida, with his wife, to visit her parents. One afternoon during his stay, he dropped into a downtown drugstore for some razor blades and saw a dozen of St. Petersburg's elderly inhabitants waiting in line at the prescription counter. Blair began chatting with them. "They were all retired, of course, and were living on their Social Security and perhaps a small pension," he recalled afterward. "The average income of those I talked to was less than a hundred dollars a month. One old fellow, a retired railroad man, who received a little more than that, told me that he had rheumatoid arthritis, and that he had to take three or four pills a day of Deltasone, Upjohn's brand of prednisone, which, like the other versions sold under trade names, retailed for thirty cents a pill. His income amounted to four dollars a day, and he spent an average of a dollar a day on Deltasone. On top of that, his wife was diabetic and had to take three Orinase tablets a day, which ran to over forty cents. The old fellow said that at the end of every month he had to give up his medicine for a couple of days so that he could afford to buy his wife's. His medicine only eased his pain, but hers kept her alive. The stories of the others were pretty much the same. There are more than ten million arthritics in the country today, most of them elderly. And old people who don't have arthritis frequently have something else that requires expensive drugs. Of course, most of them live on marginal incomes, which means that toward the end of the month they have to cut down on their drugs or their food, and when it's a matter of choosing between pain and hunger, they seem to choose the hunger."

While Blair was away, Kefauver also took a trip, spending several days resting in Hot Springs, Arkansas. One afternoon, a friend took him up twelve thousand feet in a non-pressurized airplane, and the next morning the Senator had a piercing earache. A local doctor gave him a prescription for Tetrex, Bristol-Myers' brand of tetracycline, which was the newest antibiotic on the market, and he went to a nearby drugstore to have the prescription filled. The pharmacist handed him twenty pills and asked him for ten dollars. The doctor's fee had been five dollars.

"When we both got back to Washington, Estes told me about his experience," Blair said later. "He was outraged. It had been years since he'd gone out and bought his own medicine. He had known that what we'd been telling him about prices was true, but this really brought it home to him. When he told me about it, he ended up by shaking his head and saying, 'How in the world can poor people afford to stay alive these days?' "

VII

The bread hearings wound up in July of 1959, and while Blair drew up the subcommittee's final report on that subject, his colleagues set to work to analyze the subpoenaed documents, which were now trickling in. "By late summer, we had the information we needed," Browne recalled afterward. "We had known that there was buying and selling going on, of course, but we had had no idea of the extent. For instance, we found that Schering itself produced no prednisolone but bought it under contract from Upjohn, which made forty-five per cent of all the prednisolone on the market. And then we made a discovery that stunned all of us. We found out how much—or, rather, how little—the stuff cost." The discovery came about when Dr. Till happened to notice one document showing that in a 1958 transaction Upjohn had sold Schering 251,000 grams of prednisolone for $594,870—a rate of $2.37 a gram. From this, it was easy to calculate that the cost of the material in a five-milligram tablet of Meticortelone came to slightly over a penny. The druggist paid eighteen cents for a tablet and the consumer thirty cents.

Blair went over these figures to make sure they were correct. Then, suddenly, it occurred to him that they could be used as cost figures. "By this time, we had despaired of ever getting hold of cost data," he said later. "The thought struck me, Why not use these figures, showing the margin between basic production costs and selling price? True, they included Upjohn's profit, but all that meant was that we would be using very conservative figures. The important thing was the spread between this amount and the eighteen cents the druggist paid. For our purposes, it didn't matter that the true cost figure, without Upjohn's profit, would have been a few tenths of a cent less. Moreover, in calculating true cost data we would have had to average out a figure for each step in the production process, and the industry could have attacked our conclusions at every one of those steps. This way, our case was indisputable."

Just as Blair had reached this conclusion, Browne dashed his spirits by pointing out that their figures did not include the cost of tableting and bottling the bulk powder. When Blair mentioned this problem to Mrs. Wendt, she said she dimly recalled from her work on the F.T.C. study of antibiotics that these operations were ordinarily carried out on a contract basis by a number of small companies. Blair then asked Browne to get price quotations from three firms for tableting and bottling prednisolone. When the figures came in, they were found to vary only slightly, and Blair chose the middle one—that submitted by the Richlyn Laboratories, of Philadelphia—for his calculations. Its charge for tableting and bottling was not quite half a cent per tablet in lots of a thousand, including the customary five-per-cent allowance for wastage. Adding Richlyn's charge to the approximate production cost, Blair came up with a total cost figure, including profits for both Upjohn and Richlyn, of 1.567 cents a tablet.

Blair told Dixon what the staff had found, and together they went to see Kefauver. Again, the Senator simply did not believe that the figures were accurate. "Estes insisted on examining them in infinite detail—grasping every facet and implication of them," Blair remarked afterward. "Then he asked for all the primary data—the subpoenaed documents and the letter from Richlyn—and he sat down and worked out the mathematics for himself. After that, he and Dixon went over the whole thing together. Finally, Estes agreed that the figures were correct. He knew that it was going to take some courage to make them public—not just because they were shocking but because they were irrefutable and left the industry no loophole, no way to save face. This meant that from then on the industry would be out to attack him in every possible way."

Ever since word of the drug investigation had leaked out, almost a year before, Kefauver had been under pressure to drop it. Some of the pressure had come from doctors, retail druggists, chambers of commerce, and various industries in his home state, but the most strenuous exertions had been made by the retail-drug associations, which constitute one of the most powerful political lobbies in the country. About the time that the cost figures were being compiled, a trade periodical of the food, drug, and cosmetics industries named *F-D-C Reports* and more commonly known as the Pink Sheet announced that the Senator had been so urgently reminded by Tennessee pharmacists that there was at least one of them in every town in the state that he had finally promised not to make an issue out of retail markups on drugs. However, it went on to warn the pharmacists that any attack on the drug manufacturers was bound to spill over onto them. Before long, other organs of the trade began to report that the Senator was wavering under increasing pressure from retailers, and on September 21, 1959, the *Drug Trade News* announced, "Lately there have been reports that Sen. Kefauver who faces an uphill battle for reëlection next year was being urged to drop the inquiry entirely."

The Senator had indeed been advised by various political friends to toss this potato to someone else in the Senate, and he was having difficulty in making up his mind. He and Dixon, who lived not far from each other on the outskirts of Washington, customarily drove to and from work together, and every day during this period they discussed practically nothing else in the course of the drive. "We kept going over and over it, trying to assess what the effects might be," Dixon said later. "Estes kept asking me, 'Is it right? Is it in the public interest? Does it need to be done?' After all that the staff had come up with, I couldn't answer anything but 'Yes' each time. Estes finally said, 'Well, then, we had better go ahead.' "

On September 25, 1959, Kefauver called a press conference to announce that hearings on the drug industry would begin early in December. The first of them, he said, would deal with specific products—such as the cortical steroids, antibiotics, tranquillizers, and antidiabetics. Later, the subcommittee would conduct hearings on a number of general topics, including advertising practices, generic and trade names, side effects, and the possibility that pharmaceutical companies were able to exert influence over government regulatory agencies. Perhaps the most compelling reason for starting out with the cortical steroids was that, at this stage, when less than a fifth of the over-all investigative work had been done, the cortical-steroid part was most nearly completed, and the subject illustrated a good many vital aspects of the business. The drug industry appeared to be jubilant over the choice, because, unlike many other drugs, the cortical steroids had been developed almost entirely in this country. "In selecting cortical steroids as the kickoff subject for his public hearings, the drug industry's own 'Mr. K' provided pharmaceutical execs with as good an opportunity as could be expected under the circumstances," the Pink Sheet observed. "The cortical steroid story has a number of built-in P-R plusses."

VIII "Things get very lonely in Washington sometimes," said President Woodrow Wilson during his second term. "The real voice of the great people of America sometimes sounds faint and distant in that strange city." Sometimes, though, it becomes distinct. A few days after Kefauver announced that drug hearings would be held, mail on the subject began reaching his desk in rapidly increasing amounts. The rate during the first week was a dozen letters a day; within a month it had gone up to fifty a day; and finally, after the hearings started, it reached several hundred a day. By a margin of a hundred to one, it was congratulatory. "It seems you are about the only fellow up there who will get in the Drivers Seat and do the Driving in anything concerning the little man," a retired postal clerk in Georgia wrote. While a few of the letters ran as long as eight pages, most of them were half a page of so, and one, from a woman in California, consisted of a single line—"Clean out the Rats." By and large, their contents were rather lachrymose, but some revealed rising spirits over the prospects ahead, such as one from an eighty-year-old man in Pennsylvania who had just left the hospital after a minor operation. "When I asked the hospital for an extra copy of my bill, which contained some $30 for 'take-home medicine,' which consisted of a small bottle of vitamin pills and a little cough syrup, I was asked why I wanted the extra copy," he wrote. "I said, 'For the Kefauver Committee.' I never sent it to you, but in about three days

I received a refund on the exorbitant charge for the drugs."

If the volume of mail from the public encouraged the staff, of far greater significance was the surprising number of favorable letters that came in from doctors. "The announcement of your investigation of the monopoly of drug houses was indeed heartening to us who practice medicine," one doctor wrote. Another said, "Every time I write a prescription, I want to shake your hand." A doctor in Indianapolis observed, "May I categorically state that if 99% of the publications dispatched by the drug companies to the doctors would cease tomorrow, there would not be one iota decrease in the current quality of medical care," and a doctor in Detroit simply sent the Senator a large carton containing the advertising brochures, letters, and samples that he had received over a period of just five days.

One complaint repeatedly heard from doctors was that many of the claims made for drugs were simply untrue. The first useful lead on this came from a physician in New York City, in the form of a copy of the *Medical Letter*, a four-page bi-weekly put out by a group of doctors as a non-profit medical service. The *Medical Letter* runs brief analyses of scientific literature on new drugs and therapeutics, and it carries no advertising. The publication, which had been in existence for less than a year, was unfamiliar to Blair, and he became extremely interested in its main article, which dealt with cortical steroids—specifically, with the newest one to appear, a Merck drug called dexamethasone, which was being sold under the name Decadron. "Dexamethasone . . . is being offered to the medical profession as 'the crowning achievement of the first corticosteroid decade,'" the *Medical Letter* reported, and continued, "A given dose of dexamethasone is equivalent therapeutically to a much larger dose of any of the other drugs in the group. But the smaller dosage in itself means practically nothing. The important question is whether the smaller dosage is accompanied, as claimed, by fewer and milder side effects. Evidence up to now indicates side effects with dexamethasone similar to those with other steroids."

The doctor who sent in the *Medical Letter* urged Kefauver to look into the advertising claims that Merck had made for Decadron, and Blair decided to go to New York and talk to the editors of the publication. "I learned that Decadron had been on the market for just about a year, and that already it was the biggest seller among the cortical steroids," he said later. "Since Merck had developed the first steroid, cortisone, and then had lost out to prednisone and prednisolene, apparently the company hoped to regain and keep its lead with Decadron. But from the literature that the people in New York referred me to, it appeared exceedingly doubtful whether Decadron was as superior as Merck claimed."

Accordingly, the subcommittee subpoenaed Merck's advertising and promotional material, and among the claims made in the documents it received were "All patients prefer Decadron," "No worrisome side effects attributable to Decadron have occurred as yet," "Now therapy can be established more safely, promptly, and predictably than with any other corticosteriod . . . with *patient need*, not side reactions, *the main consideration*," and "Therapeutic response highest ever reported. . . . Incidence of side effects lowest ever reported. Clinical trials confirm experimental data." In the literature cited by the editors of the *Medical Letter*, Blair found that Dr. Edward W. Boland, a noted authority on cortical-steroid therapy, who had conducted clinical tests on Decadron for Merck before it was released, had observed in a speech at a symposium held by the New York Academy of Sciences only a month after the drug went on the market, "The over-all results [of Decadron] in relation to improvement and side effects did not differ significantly from those obtained from prednisone or prednisolone in a group of similar composition and with similar duration of treatment." At the same meeting, Dr. William Dameshek, an eminent blood specialist, stated, "The introduction of dexamethasone seems to offer no particular advantages over the other corticoids in hematological disturbances."

"Everybody in the medical field knew, as we did, that many drugs have toxic side effects," Blair said afterward. "What was new to us was the way in which one company seemed to be able to get the edge on another by playing down or denying the existence of side effects. I knew from watching my brother-in-law and his wife how extremely sensitive arthritics are to any talk about drugs with fewer side effects. Naturally, they, and all other arthritics, eagerly clutched at any new drug that might be more helpful and less harmful. As we learned later on, some drug companies, through their public-relations firms, had planted articles in newspapers and popular magazines proclaiming the wonders of their new discoveries, even though they were not supposed to advertise prescription drugs directly to the lay public. Such articles prompted patients to insist that their doctors prescribe the drug they had read about. If a doctor wouldn't, the patient would often go out and find one who would."

IX

One morning shortly after the hearings were announced, Kefauver was visited in his office by Dr. Austin Smith, head of the Pharmaceutical Manufacturers Association and formerly editor of the *Journal* of the American Medical Association. Dr. Smith said he was there to ask two favors—that the subcommittee use only generic names during the hearings, so that the delicate doctor-patient relationship would not be upset—in other words, that patients would not acquire undue knowledge about what was being prescribed—and that he himself be called as the first witness. The Senator heard him out, said he would let him know his decision, and then talked the requests over with Blair and Dixon. They recommended that he turn Dr. Smith down on both counts.

"Actually, it would have been the easy way out, politically speaking, to go along with Smith," Blair said shortly after the hearings were completed. "If Estes had agreed not to use trade names, he would have got full credit from the public for acting in its interest, but in the end little or nothing would have been done to correct the abuses he had turned up. Since trade names are used almost exclusively in the industry, in all drug promotion, and even by doctors, any agreement not to use them would have turned the hearings into a farce."

As for Dr. Smith's request to testify first, Dixon, especially, was adamant in opposing that. "Senator Dirksen later accused Estes of demagoguery for not calling the P.M.A. and the A.M.A. as his first witnesses," he has said. "If he'd done it that way, he'd have got the biggest snow job in the world, and then he'd have had to turn around and bring out the real facts and cut their throats."

Politically speaking, perhaps the most cogent argument for not acceding to Dr. Smith's request was that if he had been given the floor for the first several days of the hearings, the press would have given him full coverage, but then public interest would have fallen off, and the impact of the staff's case would have been weakened, if not lost altogether. In any event, Kefauver refused both of Dr. Smith's requests, and, in Dixon's words, "the industry prepared for war."

The trade press immediately forgot that Kefauver was afraid to hold any drug hearings, because of the political dangers involved, and generally denounced his decision to go ahead with them as being, in the words of the *Drug Trade News*, "politically inspired." In time, the contention of the trade that the Senator was an out-and-out publicity hunter gained wide currency, and came to be expressed here and there in the lay press as well. "If Estes went after the drug people for political reasons, he didn't know much about politics," Dixon said later. "The very first rule of politics is never to make an enemy of an organized group. In taking on the drug industry, he also inevitably took on not only such organized groups as the A.M.A., chambers of commerce, and druggists' and businessmen's associations but a good many backward doctors as well. These drug fellows pay for a lobby that makes the steel boys look like popcorn venders. In the end, they mounted against Estes the most intense attack that I've seen in a quarter of a century in Washington. Anybody who dares seek the truth will be accused of being a persecutor. Estes was certainly accused of that, and much more. Before the hearings were over, he was even accused of spouting Socialism. We never had any intention of questioning anyone's right to make as much money as his ingenuity would allow. All we wanted to do was compare this industry with others in order to se whether there was any monopoly, and, if so, what should be done about it. Hell, all Estes ever did to rile those fellows was to raise the ugly head of free enterprise."

X That fall, Kefauver went to Tennessee on his annual fence-mending tour. Shortly before the date scheduled for the first hearings, he and his administrative assistant, a former newspaperman from Memphis named Charles Caldwell, put up at the New Southern Hotel in Jackson. "For weeks, I'd been carrying around a great, thick folder that the staff had prepared on the cortical steroids," Caldwell recalled afterward. "I'd been hoping to get a chance to sit down with Estes and go over it, so he'd be ready for the hearings, but I just couldn't get him to slow down. Day after day and night after night, I tried to squeeze in an hour or two on the folder, but there was always something more pressing. Finally, the last night we were in Jackson, which was the night before the hearings were to begin, I knew that it was then or never. You know, Estes insisted on an open-door policy. He would see anybody, at any time, for any reason. Well, he'd seen dozens of local politicians that night, along with some plain favor-seekers, and after I'd got rid of the last of them, I locked the door to our hotel suite and told him that he just had to bone up on this stuff. He was worn out, but he said he'd be with me as soon as he'd taken a shower. He went off to the bathroom, and I settled down in the sitting room and started arranging the papers. A few minutes later, I heard some voices down the hall, so I went to see what was going on. When I got to the bathroom, I found three men standing outside the shower and yelling at Estes. I'd neglected to lock the back door of the suite, and they'd just walked in. All they wanted, it turned out, was his autograph. Estes poked his head out between the shower curtains and just stared at them with that mildly surprised look of his, and said, 'Gee, I'm sorry, boys, but I don't have a pen on me.' Of course, they had one, so he stood there with the shower curtain wrapped around him and signed his name for them, and then I all but threw them out. I locked the back door and phoned downstairs to tell them not to put any calls through. We sat down at about ten o'clock, and I read to him from the file until past one. Then I started going over and over the pronunciation of chemical terms that would be used. You know, Estes couldn't remember anybody's name, and he was notorious for the hard time he had pronouncing complex words. Some of these terms were pretty far out—triamcinolone, methlyprednisolone—and I just had to get him squared away. I would pronounce each one slowly, and he'd repeat it after me. We had quite a time, laughing at ourselves and stumbling all over the place. When we finally staggered off to bed, I was convinced that he wouldn't remember a single one of them. But next morning, when the hearings opened, Estes sat there behind that big long table in the Senate Caucus Room and rattled them off as if he'd been born and raised in a pharmacy."

Part Two. THE HEARINGS

I Capitol Hill is probably the only place in the world where tourists come from hundreds and thousands of miles away to watch men read their mail. On an ordinary day, a visitor will find perhaps twenty or so representatives in the lower house and half a dozen senators in the upper—most of them sitting about idly. Periodically, someone will appear and interrupt the routine business being conducted to deliver a speech about the beauties of his home state or the virtues of an influential constituent. More often than not, the others on hand are there because they want to escape the hubbub of their offices or simply because they haven't been there for a long time and feel they ought to put in an appearance. Except on rare occasions, today's Congress is the haphazard custodian of the tradition of high debate—in Woodrow Wilson's words, "the severe, distinct, and sharp enunciation of underlying principles," which he described as "the essential function of a popular representative body." In Wilson's opinion, "the informing function of Congress should be preferred even to its legislative function"—a belief that has also fallen into decline. For one thing, most issues of the present are far more complex than those of the past. For another, many of them are highly controversial, and lately members of Congress have generally shown themselves to be disinclined to stand up and be counted—so disinclined that the last severe and distinct debate of any consequence was over the censure of Senator Joseph R. McCarthy, in 1954.

Although debate, high and low, resounded through the halls of Congress until recent years, the day-to-day legislative work has long been performed not on the floor of the Senate and the House but in their committee rooms. The committee system, Wilson said, being "shielded from all responsibility by its sneaking privacy," put things out of balance, since committee chairmen could do pretty much as they pleased. Today, the imbalance is far greater than it was in his time, for some two-thirds of the committee chairmen in both houses are Southerners who have risen to their positions through seniority and whose power, unchecked by debate, has steadily increased, making it more and more difficult for anyone outside the government to find out even what the current issues are. About the best the ordinary citizen can do is to follow the published reports of the activities of the various committees—sixteen standing committees in the Senate and twenty in the House, plus a hundred-odd subcommittees, select committees, joint committees, policy committees, conference committees, and committees on committees. Then, when he has become hopelessly muddled, he will probably pick out a political figure whose gait he finds congenial and tag along—or else forget the whole thing.

Still, a few men in Congress have managed to use the committee system—with as much publicity as they can generate—to air issues that had previously been evaded, if not ignored altogether. Of them all, Senator Kefauver was generally considered to be the most notable to appear on the congressional stage in recent years, for he was unusually skillful at using the committee as a way to persuade Americans that there were wrongs to be righted and rights to be asserted. "Kefauver is the Shakespeare of committee chairmen," one veteran observer of affairs on Capitol Hill said several months before the Senator died. "He takes the work of some Saxo Grammaticus on his staff and brings it to life for the man on the street."

Despite Kefauver's reputation among those familiar with Washington, most of the drug-industry executives who were scheduled to testify dismissed the forthcoming hearings out of hand. They were convinced—most of all by their adversary's coonskin cap and bumbling manner—that he was nothing more than a meddling hillybilly seeking some publicity. "They thought they'd come in there with all that high-priced legal and public-relations talent and mop up the floor with him," one industry lobbyist recalled later. "They simply refused to believe that he was tough and smart as hell."

II At seven minutes after ten on the morning of December 7, 1959, Kefauver called the Subcommittee on Antitrust and Monopoly to order in the lofty, marble-pillared Senate Caucus Room (the scene of the McCarthy hearings) and the first stage of the drug hearings—known as investigative hearings—officially got under way. On hand were a couple of hundred people—representatives of the drug industry, tourists, reporters and television crewmen, sixteen members of the subcommittee staff, Senators Kefauver and Wiley, and the opening witness—Francis C. Brown, president of the

Schering Corporation. Originally a German-owned firm, Schering was seized by the United States early in the Second World War and was run by the Alien Property Custodian until 1952, when a syndicate headed by Merrill Lynch, Pierce, Fenner & Beane bought it, for twenty-nine million dollars. Brown, a one-time New Deal lawyer, who was in charge of drafting the Banking Act of 1935 and later served as general counsel to the Federal Deposit Insurance Corporation, had been appointed by the Custodian to head the company while it was under government control, and he had been kept on by the new owners. The choice of Brown as the leadoff witness had greatly encouraged the industry, for he was known as an extremely able man, with a firm grasp of government practices and a sharp tongue.

Following the usual procedure, Brown read a prepared statement—dealing with the subject matter of the first round of hearings: the prices of cortical steroid drugs—which he had submitted to the subcommittee a couple of days earlier and to the press that morning. The statement began with a detailed description of how Merck had originally synthesized cortisone, and then it went on to recount how Schering had subsequently come up with prednisone and prednisolone. Ultimately, Brown got around to drug prices. "For every good compound that is found, there are many failures," he declared. "Some failures come after years of effort and hundreds of thousands of dollars of expense." The basic issue was not the price of drugs, Brown felt, but, rather, he said, "It is a matter of inadequate income," and suggested that Congress study *that* problem. Then, coming back to steroids, he concluded, "Men walking who were crippled, and working who were incapacitated, at a cost of between thirty and sixty cents a day, seems to me to be pretty reasonable."

A congressional hearing resembles a trial in that a charge and a denial are resolved—if, indeed, they *are* resolved—during the cross-examination of witnesses. However, the newspaper reporters who cover Capitol Hill, because they ordinarily have neither the time nor the space to describe a hearing closely, usually base their stories largely on the witnesses' prepared statements, perhaps adding a brief quotation or paraphrase to convey the views of the committee members. Kefauver, who had what one observer called "a genius for publicity creation," made it a point to bring out his biggest guns half an hour or so before the reporters had to leave to file their stories—ordinarily 11:30 A.M. for afternoon papers and 4:30 P.M. for morning papers.

On this occasion, Brown finished reading his statement at around a quarter to eleven, and Kefauver nodded to Dixon, who in turn called on Blair. Blair passed out mimeographed copies of a chart to the senators, other staff members, the witness, and the press. Prepared from the data that had been subpoenaed from Schering and Upjohn, the chart showed that Schering had bought prednisolone at a cost of $2.37 a gram, and that, after expenses for wastage and for tableting, bottling, labeling, and packaging, the cost of making a thousand five-milligram tablets could not have exceeded 1.567 cents a tablet—which cost the druggist 17.9 cents and the consumer 29.8 cents.

"Mr. Brown," Dixon said when Blair had finished, "you mentioned in your statement that you think thirty or sixty cents a day is a pretty reasonable price for the consumer to pay. Do you consider it reasonable on your part to charge 17.9 cents for a tablet when your cost certainly must be less than 1.6 cents?"

When Schering responded to the subcommittee's subpoenas

for its purchase-and-sale agreements with other firms, apparently Brown had been no more aware than Blair that these documents might be used to calculate approximate production costs. After looking at the chart for several moments, Brown replied that his company had many expenses besides the cost of production—"informational work" (promotion), "pioneering work" (research), "support of the distribution system" (sales), and "maintenance of . . . research" (research).

As the hearings went on, it became evident that Kefauver's preferred method of conducting them was to suggest or approve the general line of questioning to be followed at any particular session, and then leave the development of the case largely to his staff. Nevertheless, he often intervened to make a point that no one else had thought of, and he repeatedly moved in at a critical moment to restate a point in a way that would make it perfectly clear to the press. Sitting immobily, with his impassive face thrust slightly forward, he spoke in a hesitant monotone that was close to inaudible if he got too far away from his microphone. Since he was unfailingly polite and often let himself be summarily interrupted, some of the more aggressive witnesses in the drug hearings thought they could push him around. "The way Kefauver *sounded* was fatally deceptive, because witnesses often didn't realize what he was *saying*—that is, until they read the transcript," one reporter for a drug trade paper noted. "It took cold print to show how relentless the man could be." Kefauver often began an interrogation with "What I can't understand is . . ." and whenever he did, according to a lawyer for the drug industry, "the best thing a witness could do was knock over the table and hide behind it. That unchanging voice of his gave no hint of when the axe was going to fall," the lawyer added. "And his use of repetition was amazingly effective, too. He had a way of coming back to the same question again and again, and a witness would begin wondering what he had answered the last time and the time before that. All in all, I'd say that Kefauver was about the most formidable cross-examiner I've ever come up against."

On this first morning, Kefauver took over after Dixon's question to Brown. "Let's get it very clear," he said. "You buy this material from Upjohn. . . . All you do is put it in a capsule, add your brand name to it, and sell it. Presumably, this $2.37 price per gram . . . includes research costs, with some profit remaining for Upjohn. So presumably at $2.37 a gram you can produce it and include research and profit and depreciation and whatnot in it also. Upjohn could not under the law sell it to you at a loss. They must sell it to you at a profit. We have a reliable concern here that will tablet it for $2 [per thousand tablets] . . . so that your maximum cost per bottle of one hundred, which must include some research and some profit, is $1.57. Yet [you] sell it for $17.90. How do you justify that?"

Brown said, to begin with, that he refused to accept the 1.57-cent pill as accurate. (Some months later, McKesson & Robbins, Inc., which had just gone into the prednisolone business, informed the subcommittee that its production costs came to about a penny a tablet, which was being sold to the druggist for two cents and to the consumer for three cents, or one-tenth as much as Schering's product.) However, for the sake of the discussion, he went on to justify the spread—accurate or not. Schering's over-all costs, he said again, included supporting the "distribution system," and carrying out "educational," "pioneering," "trailblazing," and "research" work.

In an attempt to settle the research issue once for all, Blair pointed out that Schering, by its own admission, spent 8.5 per cent of its gross income on research, and that if the wholesale price of 17.9 cents were reduced by that percentage, the result would be 16.4 cents—still quite a markup. At that point, Kefauver rather idly asked Blair what the markup from 1.57 to 17.9 cents amounted to in terms of percentage. Blair said that it was an increase of 1,118 per cent. Suddenly, the reporters began writing furiously. Glancing at them impassively, Kefauver whispered to Blair that he would need markup percentages on some other drugs. Blair quickly calculated the percentage markup on several other Schering products and handed the figures to the Senator.

Then Blair presented another chart, which showed that between 1955 and 1958 Schering's net profits (after the 52-per-cent federal corporation tax) had varied between 23.2 and 46.9 per cent of net worth, and between 16.6 and 19.4 per cent of sales, and that in the five and a half years since Schering had become a private corporation its total net profits had exceeded the purchase price of the firm by about three million dollars.

"Everybody wants Schering or any other company to make a reasonable profit," Kefauver said to the witness. "But . . . there are these people who have to have these medicines, and many of them can't get the medicines. . . . I just meant that as a matter of public policy, it seemed that during some of this time you might reduce the price of your medicines a little bit rather than trying to garner back more than the corporation cost in five years."

"There were a great many uncertainties hanging over our company," Brown said. "Let me point out to you that the development of a product which has such a sizable impact upon the sales of a company as small as we were at that time is of itself a hazard, and these uncertainties influenced the management's decision all the way through."

Kefauver looked baffled. "All right," he said.

A few minutes later, the morning session ended. In the drug camp, as one of its people said afterward, "all was chaos and consternation."

However, one Schering aide suggested a way to turn the defense to the offense, and shortly after the subcommittee reconvened, after lunch, Brown tried it out. "I would like to ask, Mr. Chairman, if we can have an opportunity to study these charts and compilations which have been shown me by surprise today, and then answer them either personally or in writing," he said.

"Just a minute, Mr. Brown," Kefauver replied. "These charts on profits are well known to everybody. They were prepared by the Federal Trade Commission. They were published in *Fortune* magazine. You have been in business for a long, long time, and I don't like for you to say that this is a great shock to you. . . ."

Brown then attacked the citing of the 1,118-per-cent markup on prednisolone as "a headline item," and went on to point out that his company had to make high profits on some products in order to compensate for losses on others.

"Now, just where is the big bargain that you have on some other drugs?" Kefauver asked. "We will get to what you charge on some other drugs a little later on."

They got to other drugs at once, and Dixon first discussed estradiol progynon, which is used in menopausal disorders.

Schering, he declared, bought the drugs in bulk form from Roussel, a French firm, for $3.50 a gram, and sold a bottle of sixty tablets, containing altogether three one-hundredths of a gram, or 11.7 cents' worth, for $8.40—a markup of 7,079 per cent.

Again the reporters hunched over their pads. Brown retorted, "You seem wedded to a question of percentage," and added that the subcommittee's figures left out Schering's expenses for "selling," "manufacturing," "informational work," "advertising," "informing the medical profession," "development work," and "research."

"You did no research on this drug," Kefauver said. "You bought a finished product from Roussel. All you did was put it in a tablet, put it out under your name, and sell it at a markup of, 7,079 per cent."

Next, Dixon went on to a Schering product called ethinyl estradiol, a similar preparation, also bought from Roussel; in this case, Schering bought four hundred half-milligram tablets for 28 cents and sold them for $8.

"What am I expected to say?" Brown asked wearily. "I have repeated a number of times that we are engaged in an over-all operation."

Kefauver inhaled deeply on a cigarette, and said quietly, "What I can't understand is that small companies buy the same product from Roussel and sell it for $2 to $3. You sell it for $8. . . . You don't do any more to it than they do. You just buy it, put it up, and sell it; they buy it, put it up, and sell it."

So far, Brown hadn't received much help from the Republican side of the table—Wiley, a jovial, elderly man who was not cut out for the role of advocate-come-what-may, had little to offer and Dirksen was out of town—but now Peter N.

Chumbris, the senior minority counsel, spoke up. Reminding the subcommittee that Schering's current rate of profit was 16.6 per cent of sales after taxes, he said that at that rate the net return on an eight-dollar item would be $1.28, leaving an over-all cost of $6.72. If ethinyl estradiol should be sold at this price, the markup would still be 2,400 per cent, he said, which made percentages of this sort more or less irrelevant. (Chumbris's arithmetic was shaky, but not significantly.) Brown agreed, but he apparently failed to see that this was by far the most persuasive argument he could use—that regardless of particular markups, his company's current profits were 16.6 per cent of sales, which, though very high when compared to business generally, would scarcely shock the man in the street—for he all but ignored the point from then on. In any event, Chumbris's argument, Kefauver said later, had a grave flaw. It was true that the big firms' markup on certain products, and in certain circumstances, were relatively low (Kefauver had erred on this score), but taken as a whole, the markups were high enough to permit the companies to spend twenty-five per cent of the difference between gross income and production costs on advertising and promotion and still have a profit rate double that of American industry in general.

Shortly afterward, Blair presented still another chart, this one demonstrated that the four largest companies selling prednisone and prednisolone—Schering, Merck, Upjohn, and Pfizer—all charged exactly the same prices for them, and that these prices hadn't changed a penny since 1956, when the drugs were introduced.

Brown declared that the competitive situation in the pharmaceutical business required such prices.

"I have never understood this kind of a competitive system," Kefauver said. "How is it, if you want to be really competitive, you don't lower your price to get more of the business?"

"Senator," Brown answered, "we can't put two sick people in every bed where there is only one person sick."

One representative of the drug industry got up and left the room. "I never expected to hear anyone in the business testify that drugs prices were high because the number of sick people was limited," he said later.

The subcommittee then moved on to the question of how small firms could sell prednisone and prednisolone for as little as a quarter of what the big ones charged. When Dixon asked about this difference, Brown replied that Schering's overhead ran eight or ten times as high as that of the small companies. Dixon's next question had been prepared in anticipation of precisely that answer: How many detail men did Schering employ, and what were their salaries? Schering had four hundred and thirty of them, Brown said, together with a hundred in a subsidiary firm, and the salaries of the lot of them came to more than four million dollars a year. Dixon then pointed out that Schering, by its own account, spent some twenty-five million dollars a year—roughly a third of its gross income—on promotion, and asked if that did not put the small drug firm with limited funds for promotion at a hopeless disadvantage. Brown said he thought not, since the physician would prescribe drugs as he saw fit. For the time being, the question was left dangling, for neither side wanted to get down to whether doctors had been succumbing to ordinary advertising and sales pressure. Of course, Brown was not likely to question the good sense of the medical profession, and Kefauver, as he said later, felt that he had enough enemies at the moment.

After this, Dixon brought up Schering's bid for $23.63 per thousand tablets of prednisone to the M.M.S.A., and asked how the company could cut its usual wholesale price of $170 to the druggist by that amount.

"I am assuming that we also were doing what this committee is asking us to do—to compete," Brown answered. "We were trying to get some of the business. This was the price at which we had to get it."

"When we referred to the high price to the druggist, you said that you were maintaining a competitive price," Dixon reminded him. "Now, this is a considerably lower price. Are we to assume that this is competitive or non-competitive when you meet this lower price to the military?"

"Very frankly, I don't understand the question," Brown said.

When the first day's session came to an end—just after the afternoon press deadline, as it happened—Kefauver walked over to Brown, who had been joined by his daughter. With some reluctance, he introduced the girl to Kefauver. The Senator chatted with her for a few moments, and learned that she went to the same school as one of his own daughters. "You know," he said, turning back to Brown, "why don't you have your wife call mine, and we'll get together some evening?" Looking at him in amazement, Brown managed a nod, whereupon Kefauver shook hands with him and walked off.

"There was something deeply naïve about Kefauver," a witness to this encounter remarked later. "He seemed to feel that as long as he did what he felt was right, no one should be offended. I don't think he was ever quite aware that anyone—in fact, thousands of people—bitterly hated him."

III When Brown returned to his hotel that evening, he picked up a copy of the Washington *Evening Star* and saw the headline "Senators Find 1,118% Drug Markup." "I felt very sad," he said later. Undoubtedly, the next day's papers which carried stories about the afternoon session, made him even sadder. "Senate Panel Cites Markups on Drugs Ranging to 7,079%" ran a front-page headline in the New York *Times.* Elsewhere in the country, papers treated the story in much the same way. "Markup on a Drug is 7,000 Per Cent" ran a headline in the San Francisco *Chronicle,* followed by an editorial stating, "There is virtual unanimity of lay opinion that drugs . . . are shamefully overpriced, and that opinion has received what looks like formidable corroboration in the current inquiry." The Chicago *Daily Tribune* had a banner headline "Charge Drug Price Hiked Over 7,000%" (which it countered with a lengthy editorial, most of it a quotation from a speech delivered several months earlier by the president of Merck, to the effect that we had developed a large number of drugs and the Russians hadn't). The St. Louis *Post-Dispatch* considered the drug industry's contention that drugs were comparatively cheap since they saved lives, and observed, "In other words, the drug industry ought to be able to charge as much for a life-saving drug as the life it saves is worth, and anything less it charges is so much gravy for the customer." Dismissing this as "poppycock," it concluded, "The yardstick of a fair price is the cost."

Although Kefauver's staff was as impressed as one Washington reporter who referred to the Senator's "uncanny knack for lifting an idea or an issue out of the trough of neglect and placing it squarely on page one," none of them had expected the hearings to get such wide, and prominent, coverage, for the press had largely ignored the other investigations of administered prices. Dixon was perhaps the most surprised of all. "Then I realized that at some times the press is more free than at others," he said later. "The crucial point in this case was that ethical drug companies don't advertise prescription products directly to the layman through newspapers. That meant that since there was no pressure from advertisers, the papers could report whatever they wanted to."

Inevitably, this news buildup brought on a series of counterattacks from the industry. For instance, Brown accused the subcommittee of being insulting, of trying to exert thought control, of placing him at an unfair disadvantage, of besmirching his firm's reputation, of invading the privacy of his mind, and of prying into his personal affairs. (On the last point he was possibly referring to Dixon's disclosures about his profit situation. The previous year, Dixon showed, Brown had received a seventy-five-thousand-dollar salary and had exercised stock options at Schering that had netted him a quarter of a million dollars after taxes. When this was brought out, Brown faced Kefauver, and said: "The objectives you have, and the objectives which we have as a company and which I have individually I am sure are the same. This is, to improve the lot of humanity.") However, none of the counterattacks from the industry turned out to be very effective on the grass-roots level. In one national public-opinion poll taken a couple of months later, two-thirds of the people questioned favored federal control of drug prices—

a prospect that disturbed Kefauver almost as much as the prices themselves.

Senator Dirksen, who was taking a vacation—in Tennessee, of all places—read the newspaper accounts of the hearings and at once got in touch with Chumbris to find out what was going on. On January 21, 1960, when the subcommittee met for the second round of hearings—this one on tranquillizers—Dirksen was very much present. He characterized the method of arriving at what he called "these amazing mark-ups that were so freely bandied about in the press" as "terribly unobjective and unfair and completely inequitable," and added, "I must assert with all the vigor at my command that that is an unfair technique, and that I cannot tolerate it."

Kefauver, as somber as ever, heard him out. "I'm glad you brought up this issue," he said, with a tic of a smile, and proceeded to restate his position. "Senator Dirksen, of course it is not the subcommittee that creates the facts," he concluded. "If little companies are selling prednisone at 2 cents a tablet and the big companies are selling it identically at 17.9 cents, that is what they are doing."

At the time, the *New Republic* charged that Dirksen had "taken on himself the burden of defending America's medical and pharmaceutical interests for the Republican Party." Noting that Dirksen had attacked the chairman again and again, the article went on, "Milder and more limp came Kefauver's languid responses, always introduced with an infuriating pause and inquiry if the distinguished senator from Illinois were finished. Assured by the fuming Dirksen that he was temporarily through, Kefauver deprecatingly repeated his damning statistics, his voice never changing . . .

[and finally] Dirksen stopped trying to fire Roman candles into this pile of damp sawdust."

For several months it had been rumored that Dirksen was planning to give up his post on the subcommittee because of his duties as Minority Leader, but that the drug industry had prevailed on him to stick it out. Wiley, the industry was said to feel, was far too moderate, and Langer, who had died a month before the hearings began, had been a positive menace. (Before the hearings were over, Hennings had died, too, and O'Mahoney had left the Senate; they were replaced by Thomas J. Dodd, of Connecticut, and Edward V. Long, of Missouri.) Ultimately, the job of serving as industry spokesman fell to Senator Roman B. Hruska, an arch-conservative from Nebraska, who stepped into Langer's spot. According to one industry representative, Hruska was, if anything, too devoted to his task. "Instead of concentrating on the drug industry's considerable achievements and letting the ugly facts pass by as quickly and unobtrusively as possible," the man explained, "Hruska defended everything the industry had ever done and attacked the least significant criticisms of it at endless length. In the end, about all he accomplished was to plant the criticisms more firmly in the mind of the press than would have been true if he had shut up once in a while."

Kefauver was especially put out by Hruska's behavior. "In all my years in Congress, I've never encountered such harassment, obstructionism, and vilification," he said.

Throughout the hearings, and afterward, Kefauver was accused by members of the drug industry and by their friends in Congress of trying to give the impression that the percentage markups represented clear profit. He repeatedly denied this, pointing out that Blair's charts clearly showed the production costs to be "exclusive of selling and distribution costs," and, further, that Brown had time and again enumerated his company's other expenses. If the charges were misunderstood, Kefauver said, it could only be because of the newspapers' need for headlines and their readers' readiness to feel maltreated by business. The drug industry also contended that Kefauver had put it in a bad light by concentrating on its shortcomings and ignoring all that it had done for mankind. To this accusation, Kefauver replied that the industry had been given every opportunity to state its case and had been urged to submit any exhibits it wished.

Perhaps the best defense of Kefauver's approach came from an unexpected quarter—a spokesman for the professional pharmacists, who were generally opposed to the investigation but had tacitly agreed not to fight it as long as they were left out of it. Dr. Robert P. Fischelis, formerly general manager of the American Pharmaceutical Association and an occasional columnist for the *American Druggist*, attended every session of the drug hearings, and after they had been going on for two months, he wrote, "What is being built up in this investigation, stripped of all extraneous showmanship, is a well-documented record of what goes on in the 'business' of discovering, producing, and distributing drugs. This has never been done before in such a public manner." And he added, "Nor can one minimize the fact that the record is being put together from the statements of the top officials of the drug industry and from their answers to questions put to them by the senatorial committee."

However, Kefauver's approach was open to fair criticism. Congressional hearings have invariably been described by those who conduct them, including Kefauver, as nothing more or less than objective attempts to get at the truth, but the reality doesn't appear to be that simple. They are rarely unbaised. "The most notable committee investigations are seldom in point of fact 'investigations,'" Douglass Cater, the Washington correspondent of *The Reporter*, has written. "They are planned deliberately to move from a preconceived idea to a predetermined conclusion."

When Kefauver was asked, after the hearings, whether he had held them to get information or to give information, he answered, "Primarily to get information. But naturally you have to give information, too. If you hope to accomplish anything in an area as controversial as the monopoly and antitrust field, you've got to have an issue, and then you've got to stir up the people about it. Otherwise, you don't have a chance of getting a piece of progressive legislation through Congress."

Although his second point was true enough, the first was open to dispute, for his staff had asked only questions to which they knew the answers. While this is the lawyer's standard approach to any kind of legal contest—"Never let yourself in for a surprise" is the first rule of courtroom practice—it is bound to create a trial, or adversary proceeding, of a sort, and congressional hearings afford none of the traditional safeguards that attend courtroom trials. Still, if our way of conducting an investigation of this kind is less impartial than, say, England's, there are good reasons for it. Because of the strength of special-interest groups and the weakness of the consumer in this country, congressional reformers agree, they have no choice but to stir up the public. Actually, a handful of drug-industry executives told Kefauver privately that he had performed a public service. "There *were* abuses in the industry," one man said, "and they never would have been corrected if you hadn't put them in the spotlight."

In the end, the charge against Kefauver that stood up best was that, especially in the early stages, he gave witnesses little advance information on what they were going to be questioned about. In fact, even the minority members of the subcommittee were not shown the specific material to be used in a particular session until a few minutes before the session convened. The majority's defense was that the subcommittee's files were always open to the minority, but the sheer quantity of documents made it quite impossible to figure out what would be used and how. This procedure, though standard for congressional committees, is obviously open to extravagant abuse.

IV

The investigative hearings on the drug industry continued, on and off, for ten months, and about a hundred and fifty witnesses and their aides appeared before the subcommittee. To simplify matters, Kefauver limited testimony for the most part to the four groups of drugs that he had mentioned when he announced the subcommittee's plans back in September—after cortical steroids came tranquillizers, oral antidiabetics (used to supplement or replace insulin), and antibiotics. In each case, as with the steroids, Blair chose a widely sold drug and compared its production costs and its wholesale and retail prices. According to the evidence he presented, the production cost of Carter Products' Miltown, the leading mild tranquillizer, was seven-tenths of a cent a pill (to the surprise of all concerned, the president of the company confirmed this), the price to the druggist was 6.5

cents, and the price to the consumer was 10.8 cents; for Upjohn's Orinase, the largest-selling oral antidiabetic, the figures were 1.3 cents, 8.3 cents, and 13.9 cents; and for Polycycline—a form of tetracycline turned out by Bristol Laboratories (the drug branch of Bristol-Myers)—they were 1.7 cents, 30.6 cents, and 50 cents.

Then, using the data collected by the State Department, Blair showed that the American consumer was paying a good deal more for drugs than many people abroad were. Merck was selling its brand of prednisone in England, through a subsidiary, for less than half of what it charged here; various foreign concerns were selling such tranquillizers as chlorpromazine and prochlorperazine for less than a quarter of what Smith, Kline & French Laboratories got for them under the trade names of Thorazine and Compazine, and were selling meprobamate for a third of what Carter got for it as Miltown; and foreign manufacturers were selling the antidiabetic tolbutamide for less than half what Upjohn charged for it under the name of Orinase. And the same thing was true of some drugs actually made by American manufacturers in this country and then shipped abroad. For example, Eli Lilly & Co. was selling a form of penicillin in Mexico for two-thirds of its price here. Parke, Davis was selling Chloromycetin here for $5.10 per bottle of sixteen 250-milligram tablets and for as low as $2.19 abroad.

One of the subcommittee's witnesses was Admiral Knickerbocker, the director of the M.M.S.A., who testified that his agency, which is the largest buyer of drugs in the country, spent more than thirty-three million dollars for drugs and biological supplies in 1959. However, despite the M.M.S.A.'s enormous purchases, he said, the agency received extremely small discounts on patented drugs unless they happened to be so widely licensed that there were many bidders, as in the case of the tranquillizer reserpine, which CIBA, the patentholder, sold to druggists for $39.50 per thousand tablets and to the government, in the face of competitive bidding by over a dozen other companies, for as little as sixty cents. Of all the negotiations that the M.M.S.A. had had with the pharmaceutical industry, Admiral Knickerbocker said, the most exasperating involved an attempt to buy tetracycline hydrochloride through secret bids. These negotiations, he said, were carried on with Pfizer, which held the patent on the drug, and with Lederle Laboratories (a division of American Cyanamid), Bristol, Upjohn, and E. R. Squibb & Sons (a division of the Olin Mathieson Chemical Corporation), which were licensed to manufacture it.

"When the government first purchased these tablets, it paid $11 per bottle of one hundred in a procurement involving 94,176 bottles," the Admiral testified. "Six months later, in May, 1957, the unit price (from a different supplier) was still $11, even though the quantity purchased was about one-seventh that of the previous procurement. On the third procurement, nine months later, the price rose, inexplicably, to $17.24. . . . During 1958, there were three additional procurements of tetracycline hydrochloride for 93,476, 41,904, and 25,632 bottles, respectively. For the first two of these procurements, the price remained at $17.24 and for the third it was $17.15. In June, 1959, it seemed that this price 'freeze' finally had been broken when the Government was able to buy 46,512 bottles at a unit price of $14.36. But no! This 'thawing out' process was illusory, because two months later, in August, 1959, a solicitation for 28,000 bottles again produced an offered low price of $17.15 with three suppliers offering the identical price."

On one other occasion, the Admiral added, three firms submitted $17.24 bids—Lederle, Pfizer, and Squibb. Later, when Lyman Duncan, manager of Lederle, was testifying before the subcommittee, Dixon asked him how this had come about. "I had not the faintest idea, Mr. Dixon," Duncan answered. "It is very easy looking back, but in looking ahead I had not the faintest idea. Actually, I was astounded that they bid $17.24."

Another coincidence concerned the division of sales of tetracycline to the M.M.S.A. For the three-year period immediately before the hearings, Pfizer took 46.6 per cent of the business, and three of its licensees took almost all the rest—Lederle 17.8 per cent, Bristol 17.6 per cent, and Squibb 17.5 per cent, all on the basis of secret bids. The missing .5 per cent went to Upjohn. (Toward the end of the investigative hearings, Pfizer, American Cyanamid, and Bristol were indicted in the United States District Court, Southern District, in Manhattan, for violation of the antitrust laws, with Olin Mathieson and Upjohn named as co-conspirators but not defendants. The issue has yet to come to trial, but on August 11, 1963, the day that Kefauver's obituary appeared in the *Times*, a column alongside it announced that the F.T.C., in its quasi-judicial role, had unanimously found the five firms guilty of conspiring to fix prices on tetracycline. The Commission issued a cease-and-desist order, requiring them to stop fixing antibiotics prices, exchanging information on those prices, and submitting rigged bids on antibiotics.)

V If one were to awaken any one of a thousand drug executives in the dead of night and ask him where all those profits went, the answer would undoubtedly be "Research." For most of the witnesses at the hearings who used it tirelessly—and, as far as that goes, for many who heard it—the word seemed to have the force of an incantation. Among those who used it were such eminent scientists as Dr. Edward C. Kendall and Dr. Philip S. Hench, who in 1950 had shared the Nobel Prize for Physiology and Medicine with Professor Tadeus Reichstein of Switzerland for the discovery of cortisone, and who appeared at the hearings along with the president of Merck, the company that had underwritten their work. Dr. Hench described efforts of this kind as "some of the finest research that has ever been done in the whole world of medicine and science," and certainly Merck was known for sponsoring careful and distinguished research. However, other witnesses—most of them physicians of note —began by praising the American drug industry's accomplishments, and ended by dismissing some of its research claims as more important to public relations than to medicine. "Far from leading in drug progress, it appears that our industry has usually followed and often after a clear lag," testified Dr. Frederick H. Meyers, associate professor of pharmacology at the University of California Medical School. He did give the United States credit for the discovery of cortisone and other cortical steroids, and for anticoagulants, hydrazides, anterior pituitary hormones, antithyroids, and oral diuretics, but he went on to say that "most of the progress [in drug research] has come from European and

British researchers, both industrial and independent." Foreign researchers, he added, had discovered the antihistamines, synthetic morphine substitutes, new antimalarials, synthetic estrogen, almost all of the tranquillizers, oral antidiabetics, and penicillin, the ancestor of all the other antibiotics. The purpose of much of the work done by American drug firms, Dr. Meyers asserted, was "partly to exploit and market" these foreign products but "mostly to modify the original drug just enough to get a patentable derivative."

This point was made by other medical experts. One of them, Dr. Harry F. Dowling, head of the Department of Medicine at the University of Illinois College of Medicine, cited a particular case. In 1952, he said, Lilly put out a new antibiotic called erythromycin, which proved to be highly effective against staphylococcic infections. A year later, Pfizer introduced a modification, carbomycin, but this turned out to be more efficacious in the test tube than anywhere else, and was withdrawn half a dozen years later. Meanwhile, in 1956, Pfizer had made another try, coming up with oleandomycin, which, Dr. Dowling said, "has essentially the same effectiveness as erythromycin." In 1957, apparently still not satisfied, Pfizer brought out yet another variation, called triacetyloleandomycin, which, in the doctor's words, "was heralded as an important drug because the same oral dose that was used for oleandomycin produced somewhat higher concentrations of the drug in the blood." But then in 1958 Lilly came up with a propionyl salt of erythromycin that was said to produce higher antibacterial activity than any of its predecessors. However, Dr. Dowling said, "all of these attempts to produce higher blood concentrations are of doubtful benefit, since a slightly higher dose of the original drug would achieve the same results."

Several witnesses testified about another preoccupation of the industry—the practice of combining old drugs, perhaps with modifications, and patenting the result, or, at least, giving it a fancy new trade name. Dr. Maxwell Finland, an associate professor at the Harvard Medical School and an authority on antibiotics, pointed out that there were more than a hundred such mixtures on the market, and declared that it was "doubtful that any of these . . . combinations can be justified." For one thing, he explained, their use encouraged "shotgun therapy" and discouraged proper diagnosis. For another, they had not been proved to have any advantage over the same drugs taken separately (when they were taken separately, there was an advantage—dosages could be more closely controlled). And, finally, some of them did outright harm. He concluded by saying, "As a teacher and one who has worked hard in this field, I am naturally discouraged and disturbed that these combinations continue to be prescribed by physicians in spite of repeated expositions of their potential and actual dangers by most of the leading workers in this field." As a number of other witnesses pointed out, it was small wonder that the individual practitioner wasn't always able to keep up with these warnings, for some four hundred new drug products reached the market every year—of which, one medical witness stated, perhaps six were worthwhile.

As the hearings continued, Kefauver brought on several former drug-company employees, including a number of doctors. One of these, Dr. A. Dale Console, who had been Squibb's medical director for five years, remarked that the companies were always talking of the great number of research failures they had for every success, and said, "This is true, since it is the very essence of research. The problem arises out of the fact that they market so many of their failures."

Kefauver asked him if, in his opinion, much of the industry's research led to the marketing of drugs that were useless or worse.

"I think more than half is in that category," Dr. Console answered. "And I should point out that with many of these products it is clear while they are on the drawing board that they promise no utility. They promise sales."

Seymour N. Blackman, the executive secretary of the Premo Pharmaceutical Laboratories, a small firm with a relatively ambitious research program, remarked in his testimony that the National Institutes of Health, a government outfit, spent over a hundred and forty million dollars a year on research grants, a sum that almost equaled the research expenditures of the entire drug industry, and added that private foundations, universities, charitable organizations, and the ordinary citizen contributed far more than either. "The funds necessary for the development of the Salk vaccine were contributed mainly by public donations," he said. "The profit from the fifty-three-million-dollar sales [of the vaccine], at wholesale level, were shared by only five large drug concerns."

VI

Article I, Section 8, of the Constitution gives Congress the power "to promote the progress of science and useful arts, by securing for limited times to authors and inventors the exclusive right to their respective writings and discoveries." Some of the Founding Fathers, it appears, were rather uneasy about the patent system that Congress later created, allowing an inventor seventeen years of exclusive rights over his product. Franklin refused a patent on his famous stove, and Jefferson refused a patent on his hemp-brake, pointing out that to the best of his knowledge the only country that granted a patent on just about anything was England and that "nations which refuse monopolies of invention are as fruitful as England in new and useful devices." Using information gathered by Mrs. Wendt and Mrs. Goodwin, both of them attorneys on the subcommittee staff, Kefauver's aides prepared a table showing that at least as far as drugs were concerned Jefferson was on the right track: Countries that refused to grant patents on drugs had created just as many new drugs as countries that granted such patents. Moreover, the prices of twelve major drugs in countries with patent protection were from 18 to 255 per cent higher than the prices of the same drugs in countries without it. Some months before the hearings started, Kefauver had concluded that the antibiotics constituted the clearest illustration of monopoly power resulting from patents. A perusal of documents put into the record in the course of the hearings convinced the Senator that patents could be used not only for monopoly purposes but for economic oligopoly as well—which, he felt, was just as restrictive, when it came to the consumer, as monopoly itself. In the majority report on the investigative hearings that Blair prepared, with the assistance of his staff, and that Kefauver submitted to the Second Session of the Eighty-seventh Congress, the history of the patent fight over tetracycline—the widest selling antibiotic, which was manufactured by three leading drug firms and sold by five, was explored at length:

The moves and countermoves of the companies were of an almost incredible complexity. Accord was difficult to come by since the companies involved correctly anticipated that the stakes were extremely high. Moreover, it was touch-and-go whether the product was even patentable. To the intense distress of the companies, it developed that some quantities of tetracycline are obtained in the production of chlortetracycline [Aureomycin]—a fact which might well make the product unpatentable. The problem was further aggravated by laboratory and clinical tests which appeared to indicate that tetracycline is superior to its patented predecessors—chlortetracycline and oxytetracycline [Terramycin]. Under these circumstances the prospects of a repetition in the broad spectrums of what was so widely deplored in penicillin—free competition, falling prices, and shrinking profit margins—appeared very real indeed.

It was against this background that the companies made their legal maneuvers with the twofold objective in mind—to assure the issuance of a patent and to secure the patent for themselves. The first step was the filing of a patent application by Pfizer in September, 1952. This was followed by a similar application by American Cyanamid in March, 1953, and one by a small company, Heyden Chemical Co., in 1953.

Shortly thereafter this number was reduced to two. Less than 6 weeks after Heyden announced that it had filed an application for tetracycline, its antibiotics division was purchased by Cyanamid. Cyanamid paid $600,000 in excess of the book value of the assets of the Heyden antibiotics division—at a time when the industry was suffering from excess capacity in antibiotics production, when selling prices from penicillin and streptomcyin were extremely low, and profits on this business were falling.

On January 11, 1954, Pfizer and Cyanamid entered into an agreement. They agreed to make a private determination of priority in the invention, to the end that the loser would withdraw and thus end the interference [proceedings at the Patent Office]. It was stipulated that the winning party was to license the other.

In the meantime, Bristol had also filed a patent application on a commercial form of tetracycline; namely, tetracycline hydrochloride. The Patent Office then declared another interference on tetracycline hydrochloride on March 2, 1954, involving Pfizer, Cyanamid, and Bristol as the parties. By this time Cyanamid had already filed formal concession in the earlier interference, yielding priority to Pfizer. Bristol then approached Pfizer for a license, but was turned down.

Almost immediately—on April 30, 1954—Bristol entered the market with its own tetracycline. A number of companies—including Upjohn, Squibb, Smith Kline & French, and Parke, Davis—sought to purchase the bulk material from Bristol. Of these, Upjohn and Squibb were selected by Bristol to sell its tetracycline production in addition to itself.

Although, under the earlier private agreement between Cyanamid and Pfizer, it was Pfizer who was to get the tetracycline patent, the latter could not act since no patent had yet been issued. Cyanamid then moved into the breach; on September 29, 1954, it instituted action against Bristol on the ground that Bristol's manufacture of tetracycline infringed Cyanamid's Aureomycin patent. This turned out to be strategically sound, for a month later, on October 14, 1954, the examiner in the Patent Office dissolved the second interference. He stated that since tetracycline had been produced in the manufacture of Aureomycin, the product was old, had been sold in the market, and was therefore unpatentable. Had this decision stood, what has turned out to be the country's largest selling broad-spectrum antibiotic would have been marketed as an unpatented drug.

Pfizer, however, persisted in its submission of affidavits to overcome the rejection by the patent examiner, who asked if tetracycline could be shown to be present in Auremycin "in clearly identifiable form." Pfizer scientists conducted tests purporting to prove that Aureomycin fermentation broth did not contain tetracycline. Using what Pfizer itself described as "low potency" broth and "commercial" tests, a negative result was secured, although the use of known sensitive tests would have shown the presence of identifiable tetracycline in the broth. In an affidavit submitted to the Patent Office, the Pfizer scientist swore that "in fact there was no indication whatever of the presence of tetracycline." This led the patent examiner to grant the patent to Pfizer. On the same day separate infringement actions were instituted by the patentee against Bristol, Upjohn, and Squibb.

This set the scene for the end of the matter. On January 13, 1955, Cyanamid's infringement action against Bristol was settled with a license by Cyanamid for use of its Aureomycin patent in the manufacture of tetracycline. In return, Bristol agreed to pay royalties to Cyanamid on all of its sales of tetracycline. A month later, on February 25, 1955, Bristol formally moved to abandon its patent application still pending in the Patent Office, on the ground that the product claims were unpatentable. This left only the Pfizer infringement suits to be disposed of. For another year, litigation continued. Pfizer pressed its action. Bristol, Upjohn, and Squibb counterclaimed with charges of lack of invention, prior use, and misrepresentation of the facts in the Patent Office.

Then suddenly the controversy was stilled. In March, 1956, the six lawsuits then pending were privately settled in a series of agreements among the companies. Squibb and Upjohn were licensed by Pfizer merely to sell, but not to manufacture, tetracycline. In addition to paying a lump sum for infringement, Bristol received a license from Pfizer for the manufacture and sale of tetracycline with the payment of royalties. In turn Pfizer was granted access to any Bristol patents in this field; if it exercised this option, Pfizer was obligated to pay royalties to Bristol.

With the consummation of these arrangements, the orderly and controlled marketing of tetracycline was an inevitable and expected result.

At the time that the F.T.C. issued its cease-and-desist order, it observed that "unclean hands and bad faith played a major role" in the private settlements.

VII

In the belief that doctors are experts who cannot be fooled, Congress specifically exempted advertising directed at the medical profession from the F.T.C. Act of 1914, which gives the Commission regulatory power to prohibit false and misleading advertising in interstate trade. At the Kefauver hearings, several witnesses suggested that doctors not only could be but were being fooled. Dr. Solomon Garb, a member of the faculty of the Albany Medical College, described a course he had conducted in which his students evaluated various kinds of drug advertising. Although the material sent out by some drug companies was exemplary, he said, "the majority of the mailed ads were unreliable, to the extent that a physician trusting them could be seriously misled."

One advertising campaign that was referred to in the hearings promoted a tranquillizer called Deprol, which was produced by Wallace Laboratories, a division of Carter. "Deprol helps balance the mood by lifting depression as it calms related anxiety," a typical claim stated. In the opinion of most medical men, no drug should be put on the market until it has been clinically evaluated and test results have been published by a number of researchers. Dr. Heinz Lehmann, a Canadian psychiatrist who is one of the world's leading authorities on tranquillizers, testified that Deprol had been widely advertised on the basis of a single medical-journal article—an article that had not even been published when the promotional campaign for the drug was begun. "There is not much to substantiate the first early claims of its efficacy in depressions," he concluded.

Another psychiatrist, Dr. Fritz Freyhan, who was then director of research at the Delaware State Hospital, also testified on Deprol. He pointed out that the general practitioner "cannot and should not be expected to be so familiar with the symptomatology of depressions. . . . He is, however, told that depression per se, all depressions, can be treated with this drug, and this is not true and it has not been shown to be the case in an authoritative article, I think it is fair to say. The very intensive Deprol promotion campaign which reaches my desk at least two or three times a week really makes me feel quite concerned about what may happen to depressed patients who are treated by the general practitioner."

In his testimony, Dr. Console had characterized the pharmaceutical industry as "unique in that it can make exploitation appear a noble purpose." An abundance of myths had been created, he said—among them the myth that advertising was a kind of postgraduate education for the physician. He noted that in medical school the student was taught to seek the cause of, say, a fever and that most drug advertising ignored the cause and harped on the cure—the company's product. In the course of one promotional campaign that he recalled, the manufacturer had sent him a clinical thermometer along with a sample of its drug. "The invitation is delightfully tempting," he said. "Too many physicians, pressed for time, would like to believe that medicine can be practiced with a thermometer and a bottle of pills."

Dr. Console, like several other expert witnesses, also declared that a large number of the drugs then being marketed were useless, and he added that a claim persistently made by the industry—that it could police itself—was nonsense. Under the law, the F.D.A. could, except in a few instances, bar a drug only if it was unsafe, and not if it was inefficacious. However, as a former F.D.A. medical officer pointed out at the hearings, "No drug is safe if it fails to cure a serious disease for which a cure is available."

One witness for the industry contended that the job of making and selling drugs was far different from that of making and selling automobiles. Dr. Console concurred. "If an automobile does not have a motor, no amount of advertising can make it appear to have one," he said. "On the other hand, with a little luck, proper timing, and a good promotion program, a bag of asafetida with a unique chemical side chain can be made to look like a wonder drug. The illusion may not last, but it frequently lasts long enough. By the time the doctor learns what the company knew at the beginning, it has two new products to take the place of the old one."

All the way through, Senator Hruska was much exercised by this kind of talk, and he accused some of the doctors who testified along such lines of impugning their colleagues' integrity—or, at any rate, competence. "The Republicans on the subcommittee made repeated efforts to turn the criticism of advertising into a reflection on the intelligence of the doctors, apparently in the hope of arousing the American Medical Association," reported the Public Affairs Institute, a non-profit Washington research organization. "Many of the experts refused to be frightened, however, and said frankly that large numbers of doctors are taken in—as indeed would appear undeniable in view of the vast success of the advertising."

One doctor who was neither taken in by drug advertising nor frightened by Hruska was Charles May, professor of pediatrics at the New York University School of Medicine, editor of *Pediatrics,* and a member of both the A.M.A.'s Council on Drugs and the New York Academy of Medicine's Committee on Pharmaceutical Advertising. He delivered a strong indictment of the drug industry's advertising practices, which Hruska tried to turn into something quite different:

SENATOR HRUSKA: You suggested that the patient was being mistreated. That is an indictment of the medical profession, is it not, Doctor? . . . Does a physician depend on advertisements or this literature that he gets in the mail to decide whether he is going to prescribe for a patient? Does he say, "Now here is an advertisement that says it is going to cure my patient, therefore I am going to prescribe it"? Is that the way, in your experience, physicians go about selecting a given drug?

DR. MAY: There are studies of this question by a group of sociologists at Columbia University, in the Bureau of Applied Social Research, in which they studied the manner by which physicians learn of a new drug, and it is composed of several means: person-to-person contacts, reading of basic scientific literature, material garnered from advertisements and promotional material, and contact by detail men. There were several vectors, of which promotion material was certainly one.

SENATOR HRUSKA: And that is how they learn about a new drug?

DR. MAY: Yes, sir.

SENATOR HRUSKA: I still return to my question: Does a doctor, when he prescribes a drug, do it as the result of reading an advertisement and saying, "My, my, this wonderful description of the drug in the ad that I got in today's mail just fits Mrs. Jones's case. Therefore, I will prescribe this for Mrs. Jones." Do you think that is the way doctors in America prescribe for their patients?

DR. MAY: If you are attempting to lead me into condemning physicians on the basis of their being influenced by this promotional material—

SENATOR HRUSKA: Wait a minute! I am not trying to lead you into anything. I am asking you a question. You are an authority on this subject. You have said here that they depend upon authenticity of the claims, and to the detriment of the patient, and that patients have been mistreated. Now, all I ask you is to confirm, so that I won't misunderstand, that these advertisements form the basis for a doctor's prescribing for his patients.

DR. MAY: I would suggest that the sales of drugs—

SENATOR HRUSKA: You have referred to a study of methods whereby doctors learn about new drugs.

DR. MAY: Yes, sir.

SENATOR HRUSKA: You have now referred to the increased sale of drugs. I still return to my question.

DR. MAY: Yes, sir.

SENATOR HRUSKA: When a physician prescribes for his patient, does he do it on the basis of the advertisements in the magazines and in this independent direct mailing which he receives?

DR. MAY: I think there are unquestionably times when he does do so.

SENATOR HRUSKA: There are times when he does do so?

DR. MAY: Yes, sir.

SENATOR HRUSKA: And how many times does he do so?

DR. MAY: I was about to introduce this statement previously by saying the sales of these drugs suggest it must be quite frequently. . . . I am not contending that the physician depends exclusively upon this material at all times. I am contending that this is put before him as a major source of information, that it is an influential body of promotional material, and thus it is imperative that the information which reaches the physician from whatever source is as accurate as it possibly can be. . . .

SENATOR KEFAUVER: Dr. May, as I understand it, you are not contending, and you do not contend in your statement, that advertising and promotion is the only thing that a doctor uses in prescribing. You say that he secures all the information available from all sources, as I understand it. Is that correct?

DR. MAY: Yes, sir.

SENATOR HRUSKA: If that is the fact, I think that is wonderful, because that is the point I tried to establish.

If the quality of drug advertising was not always impressive, the quantity certainly was. One of the documents read into the record was a statement made to the American College of Apothecaries in 1959 by Walter L. Griffith, director of product advertising and promotion for Parke,

Davis, noting that during the previous year "the ethical pharmaceutical industry of this country" had turned out "3,790,908,000 pages of paid journal advertising" and "741,213,700 direct-mail impressions," and that its detail men had made between eighteen and twenty million calls on physicians and pharmacists. Kefauver had subpoenaed the records of the twenty-two largest manufacturers relating to their expenses for 1958 advertising and promotion, and these showed that $580,000,000, or an average of twenty-four per cent of the companies' gross income, had gone for those purposes. On the basis of these figures, the subcommittee staff estimated that in the same period the whole industry must have spent at least three-quarters of a billion dollars to sell its wares.

One recipient of the usual drug-company mail who testified before the subcommittee was Dr. James E. Bowes, an obstetrician from Salt Lake City, who had become so annoyed by the sheer volume of circulars and samples pouring into his office daily that he had got hold of a postal scale and had weighed every piece of material he received over a two-month period. "The results soon began to look fantastic," he reported. "It would take two railroad cars, one hundred and ten large mail trucks, and eight hundred postmen to deliver the daily load of drug circulars and samples to doctors if mailed to a single city." Another physician stated that there was no way to avoid the avalanche, either. Like many of his colleagues, he said, he had told his secretary to throw away all drug mail, but one company, apparently alerted to this order by its detail man in the area, started sending its material to the doctor under first-class postage with the name and address of its medical director on the corner; as soon as the doctor caught onto that, they sent their advertisements to him air mail; and, finally, when that, too, failed, they mailed them to him from abroad. "Any device, regardless of expense, will be used to overcome the physician's resistance," he said.

This vast promotional effort, Kefauver concluded, had essentially one purpose—to plant trade names firmly in the minds of physicians. The situation was unique in the world of commerce, for, as he remarked during the hearings, "he who orders does not buy, and he who buys does not order." Once a doctor has written a trade name on a prescription blank, the patient is stuck. For one thing, even if there is a cheaper equivalent available, pharmacists in four-fifths of the states are forbidden by law to substitute it, and, for another, trade-named drugs ordinarily sell for the same price in every drugstore.

About the only industry witness who agreed with Kefauver was Premo's Blackman, who had also testified on research. "The only real competition that we have in our field," he testified, "is the tremendous competition for the eye and ear of the physician—how many pages of advertising we can put out, how many samples we can distribute, how many detail men we can put in the field. These, and these alone, govern the ultimate acceptance of the product." Some years earlier, he went on, his firm had done its best to break into the big time by splurging, relatively speaking, on detail men and advertising. However, he said, his company's gross income—two million dollars a year—was about what one of the large manufacturers spent in getting a single product off the ground. In the end, Premo's effort amounted to little more than what Blackman called "a spark in a vast conflagration"—a spark that quickly spluttered and died out. One example of Premo's failure to succeed involved its penicillin, which it sold for $3.75 a hundred tablets, without many buyers, while Squibb was doing rather well with the same preparation, under the name Pentids, at $14.85 a hundred.

In 1958, a survey made for the A.M.A. revealed that detail men were the single most important source of medical information on drugs as far as doctors were concerned, sixty-eight per cent of whom regarded their visits as the most effective way of keeping up on new developments. The A.M.A. could have saved itself the cost of the survey by simply asking the larger manufacturers how many detail men they used and what they paid them—fifteen thousand in all, the hearings revealed, or one for every ten practicing physicians in the country, with total annual salaries of some two hundred million dollars. According to much of the testimony, they clearly earned their money. Dr. Garb, for instance, told how he had spent many months teaching his students to prescribe by generic name whenever possible, only to have one-half of them decide that trade names were preferable—after a single session with a detail man. The basic maxim of detail men, Dr. Console said, was "If you can't convince them, confuse them," and many other medical witnesses who testified agreed that drug salesmen were scarcely the high-minded class that the industry claimed. "The physician, if he is uncertain of what his fellow physicians may be doing, does not want to be left at the post in any new therapeutic race," one doctor remarked. "So, with the reassurance he gets, the new therapy is launched. The results are variable but not all according to the spiel."

Blackman, who had hired his share of detail men when Premo tried to break into the big time, was somewhat more emphatic:

SENATOR HART: [Say that] I am running a streak of bad luck and I am sick. I go to a doctor. The doctor has been called upon by your detail man. As a patient am I luckier that he has been called on by detail men or not? . . .

MR. BLACKMAN: I would say not necessarily, and probably not. . . . I feel that to a certain extent the doctor has been had. He relies [on] and confides in these detail men. They are neither his confidant, his friend, nor his professor at school. They are pure, unadulterated salesmen.

SENATOR HART: Is that what you sought when you hired them?

MR. BLACKMAN: Absolutely.

In the view of an F.D.A. physician who followed the hearings closely but was not called upon to testify, the medical experts who objected to detail men were by no means representative of his profession. "Plenty of doctors are crazy about detail men," he explained. "In small towns, they not only bring doctors free samples and information but open up their bags and give them presents of all sorts —desk sets, expensive calendars, elaborate medical charts, illuminated anatomy figures, monogrammed golf balls, and so on. They're regular Santa Clauses. And they also bring news from other towns on the circuit. When you come down to it, they're very much like old-fashioned drummers, and plenty of doctors look forward to their visits. This is not to say, however, that they do anything to advance the cause of medicine."

Ordinarily, a drug has three names: the chemical name, which simply lists its components; the generic name, which is customarily an abbreviated description of the components; and the trade name. The chemical name is fixed, and the trade name is entirely up to the manufacturer as long as it doesn't conflict with another brand. At the time, though, a company could give a drug any generic name it chose, subject to lenient restraint by one or another semi-official agency. In the course of the hearings, it became clear that some generic names failed to indicate the drugs' chemical structure, that in quite a few cases a drug had different generic names, and that some drug companies at least gave the impression of going to great lengths to devise generic names that even a professor of pharmacology would boggle at. As examples of generic complexity and trade simplicity, one doctor cited chlordiazepoxide, or Librium; isocarboxazid, or Marplan; piperidolate hydrochloride, or Dactil; and thioridazine hydrochloride, or Mellaril. Another witness, discussing a new form of synthetic penicillin that had recently been put out by six companies, noted that the substance had ended up with one chemical name (alpha-phenoxy-ethyl penicillin potassium), three generic names (potassium penicillin-125, phenethicillin potassium, and the chemical name), and six trade names (Alpen, Chemipen, Darcil, Dramcillin-S, Maxipen, and Syncillin), and that it had appeared on the market under all these trade names, and in a variety of shapes and colors, within a period of two months. It also turned out that a drug was sometimes given more than one name so that it might be recommended for more than one use.

Dr. Walter Modell, associate professor of pharmacology at the Cornell University Medical College and editor of *Drugs of Choice*, a physicians' manual, told the subcommittee that "no practicing physician can possibly deal with this Hydra-headed monster of terminology." As he saw it, the proliferation of names created two problems. One was "the danger of not giving the patient the best drug available." The second, he observed, after noting that one drug he knew of had as many as twenty-five names, was that "if a patient is allergic to a drug under one trademark name, and the doctor, in trying to avoid it, gives him the same drug under another trademark, because he doesn't know that the two are identical, he can cause a catastrophe."

Representatives of the M.M.S.A., state and municipal welfare agencies, and hospitals and clinics testified that they bought drugs on a generic-name basis whenever they could. Also, more and more hospitals seemed to be using the formulary system—under this, attending physicians give their written permission to the hospital pharmacist to substitute equivalent drugs for any trade-marked item they prescribe. By this means, Dr. August H. Groeschel, associate director of New York Hospital, testified, his hospital had managed to save a quarter of a million dollars a year by stocking only three hundred and fifty-nine drugs to treat all known illnesses. While large hospitals and the M.M.S.A. had laboratories where they could test generic-named drugs, it was pointed out at the hearings, individual doctors obviously didn't have such facilities. Clearly, most of the drugs sold under generic names were dependable (the small houses almost invariably bought finished bulk powder, such as prednisone, from the big ones), but a few so-called bathtub operators did turn out substandard drugs, and it was impossible for a doctor on his own to know which of the thousand small concerns were trustworthy. As Drs. Blair and Till had discovered earlier, the ordinary practitioner almost invariably decided to depend on the reputation of a manufacturer, which, of course, meant ending up with one of the giants. As a colloquy between Dixon and Dr. Groeschel indicated, the physician was concerned not just about his patients:

MR. DIXON: In other words, if the doctor prescribed a drug product, relying upon that drug product, the drug company cannot escape liability.

DR. GROESCHEL: No.

MR. DIXON: It is not just the doctor?

DR. GROESCHEL: I think it is under the law of product warranty, I believe.

MR. DIXON: Yes.

DR. GROESCHEL: Yes, indeed. And the bigger the company, the more comfortable I expect the doctor would feel.

VIII

The hearings revealed that although practically all drugs had adverse side effects on certain poeple under certain conditions, not all drug manufacturers had posted warning signs. At Kefauver's request, the Library of Congress had made a survey of the advertisements for thirty-four widely used trade-named drugs that appeared in six prominent medical journals during the months between July, 1958, and March, 1959. In all, the study covered more than two thousand pages of advertisements, and found that eighty-nine per cent of the ads either contained no mention of side effects or dismissed them briefly. The current law stated that each shipment of a new drug must contain as a package insert a small folder giving complete details on a drug, and that this document, unlike drug advertising, had to be approved by the F.D.A. The insert, however, had to be sent not to the physician but to the pharmacist, which meant, as Kefauver pointed out, that it usually ended up in a drugstore wastebasket. Moreover, he observed later, evidence collected by the subcommittee showed that "many of the nation's largest commercial banks and investment companies, in deciding how to invest funds, attach great importance to what they hear about a new drug's side effects." And, finally, as Dr. David P. Barr, president and medical director of the Health Insurance Plan of Greater New York, testified, five per cent of all the patients in hospital wards were being treated for ailments resulting from doctors' treatments, particularly from side effects of drugs—a situation, he declared, that made the problem equivalent to a major disease.

In preparing for the hearings, Kefauver's staff looked into the side effects of, among other drugs, the oral antidiabetics. The first of these, tolbutamide, was developed in Germany and licensed by a firm called Farbwerke Hoechst to Upjohn, which began selling it here, very successfully, under the name of Orinase. Not long afterward, Pfizer came up with a related drug, to which it gave the generic name chlorpropamide and the trade name Diabinese. In its advertisements, Pfizer told physicians, variously, that Diabinese was "the oral antidiabetic most likely to succeed," that it had an "almost complete absence of unfavorable side effects," and that it would "eventually prove to be the drug of choice in the sulfonylurea group." At the time of the hearings, about sixty thousand Americans were taking Diabinese.

John E. McKeen, president and chairman of the board of Pfizer, giving the subcommittee a document in which thirty-six doctors endorsed Diabinese, testified that the drug had been investigated with great care. Blair, however, had received a tip that made him dubious on this point, and he was eager to get his hands on two other documents that dealt with the clinical studies on Diabinese; both of them, he had been told, were prepared by Dr. Domenic G. Iezzoni, Pfizer's associate director of clinical research. Despite repeated requests to Pfizer for this material, Blair has said that he obtained neither document until early on the morning of McKeen's appearance, when they were slipped under his office door. A quick look showed that they had been well worth waiting for. In one, Dr. Iezzoni's data showed that the incidence of side effects had amounted to twenty-seven per cent. In the other, a memorandum addressed to McKeen personally, the doctor had written, in part:

> Our study program with Diabinese in patients with diabetes mellitus is continuing. Approximately 1,200–1,500 persons have been given this medication (domestically) either for the control of their diabetes or as part of testing programs. . . .
>
> In the evaluation of Diabinese we have encountered an incidence of toxicity which, at the least, is not less than that seen with Orinase. We have encountered six cases of jaundice. The jaundice in each instance developed after 3 to 4 weeks of chronic daily treatment with Diabinese. . . . It is significant that subsequent to their jaundice, two of these patients, after being on Orinase for 4 weeks, and one patient, after being on Orinase for 2 weeks, do not, at present, show any clinical or laboratory evidence of liver toxicity. . . .
>
> Among the most striking evidences of toxicity associated with Diabinese are three instances of exfoliative dermatitis [extensive scaling, itching, and redness of the skin, along with loss of the hair]. . . . There have been reported several additional cases of severe skin eruptions with edema [abnormally large amounts of fluid in the skin] and erythema multiforme [an acute skin affliction with burning papules and tubercules] in addition to the other skin lesions. . . .
>
> The gastrointestinal side effects of nausea, vomiting, and epigastric distress, although less frequent at the lower dosage levels of 0.25–0.5 gm./day, are still more frequent than generally noted with Orinase. . . . There have been several instances of severe hypoglycemia [subnormal glucose in the blood] in patients receiving doses as low as 0.25–0.5 gm./day. No death has occurred

from hypoglycemia at these lower dose levels. One patient, however, died of intractable hypoglycemia following Diabinese medication.

Among other complaints still evident at the lower doses are such things as headaches, hazy vision, depression, weakness, and three cases of eosinophilia [an excessive accumulation of one kind of cell in the blood].

Of the side effects noted with Diabinese medication the jaundice and exfoliative dermatitis are particularly outstanding when one realizes that, to date, there has been no reported instance of either of these complications in patients treated with Orinase.

After Dr. Iezzoni's memoranda were put into the record, Dirksen and Hruska denounced Kefauver to the press for attempting to evaluate the worth of a particular drug, and McKeen begged Kefauver not to continue. "May I . . . plead with you, Senator," he said, "in the interest of the public welfare and the peace of mind of those thousands safely taking our drug that you cease dealing with medical aspects of the drug, which are, quite candidly, apparently beyond the depth of this committee."

Kefauver was not moved. "I believe that patients ought to be cautious," he told McKeen. "I think the evidence here and in other places justifies the patient in asking about side effects. . . . Perhaps getting the truth out will cause the pharmaceutical manufacturers, who are not giving all of the facts, to understand the importance of doing so."

Probably no other profession has quite the prestige of medicine—partly, no doubt, because no other profession is so closed off from criticism. No one outside the field is competent to evaluate its practices, and exceedingly few within it are willing to. Some, though, will discuss it in private, and a veteran F.D.A. doctor recently attributed most of the abuses of the drug industry to the quality of medical education. "The trouble is that doctors are even more pill happy than their patients," he explained. "Too many of us are looking for the magic formula, the total cure. The pharmaceutical manufacturers find one every week, and there are plenty of doctors who are willing to try it out. One of the greatest problems any doctor faces is that three-quarters of his patients are neurotic, not physiologically sick. Most doctors just don't want to deal with patients like these any more than they have to, so they prescribe the latest pill and get rid of them. That way, they make a lot more money with a lot less work—even if the pill isn't worth a damn or shouldn't be given to that particular patient."

The best illustration of the latter in recent years, the doctor went on, was the misuse of antibiotics, especially of Parke, Davis's Chloromycetin—or chloramphenicol, generically speaking—a highly potent medicine and also an exceedingly worthy one. According to a 1961 report in the *Medical Letter*, a non-profit publication on drugs put out in New York by a group of well-known doctors and pharmacologists, it is regarded as the drug of first choice for typhoid and Hemophilus influenza meningitis, and possibly also for coliform peritonitis and Klebsellia pneumonia. The report quoted the eminent hematologist, Dr. William Dameshek, who had written that eight of thirty patients suffering from aplastic anemia whom he had seen in the past three years had had "significant" dosages of chloramphenicol and that "the tragic thing about all these . . . cases, most of whom died, is that the drug need never have been given." The *Medical Letter* piece concluded, "Even though serious reactions are infrequent, there is little point in risking its toxic and sensitizing potential in the treatment of upper-respiratory infections or in infections for which equally effective and safer antibiotics are available."

The story of Chloromycetin was an interesting one. Back in 1951, Parke, Davis had sold fifty-two million dollars' worth of the drug (which put the company at the top of the industry in earnings for that year), and this figure, the F.D.A. man said, had made it clear that doctors were prescribing it for just about everything. That same year, though, word began to spread that Chloromycetin had been associated with a number of blood dyscrasias (abnormal states of the blood)—including aplastic anemia. The 1951 issue of *New and Non-Official Remedies,* a compilation published by the American Medical Association's Council on Drugs, warned that "changes in the peripheral blood or the blood-forming organs have been reported during the use of chloramphenicol." Then, in June of 1952, an editorial in the *Journal* of the A.M.A. stated, "In the experience of one group, this anemia [aplastic] has occurred in patients who have previously received one or more courses of chloramphenicol without untoward effect. When the drug was subsequently administered, even in small doses, a severe blood abnormality has appeared. Even deaths have been reported."

Before the end of the month, the F.D.A., which was empowered to certify, and de-certify, the use of the first antibiotics, suspended certification of chloramphenicol and turned the problem over to a committee appointed by the National Research Council. Soon afterward, the F.D.A. reported, "the committee considered the records of 410 serious blood disorders, of which 177 were definitely known to have been associated with the use of Chloromycetin." The F.D.A. nevertheless decided to let Parke, Davis go on selling the drug, explaining that "the Administration has weighed the value of the drug against its capabilities for causing harm and has decided that it should continue to be available for careful use by the medical profession in those serious and sometimes fatal diseases in which its use is necessary," but it ordered the company to print the following warning at the top of each package insert:

> Certain blood dyscrasias (aplastic anemia, thrombocytopenic purpura, granulocytopenia, and pancytopenia) have been associated with the administration of Chloromycetin. It is essential that adequate blood studies be made when prolonged or intermittent administration of this drug is required. Chloromycetin should not be used indiscriminately or for minor infections.

By 1955, Parke, Davis was not doing so well with Chloromycetin. Its sales had fallen to a mere thirty-five million dollars. But in 1960, the year that Harry J. Loynd, the company's president, appeared before the subcommittee, they were higher than ever—some eighty-six million. Kefauver questioned Loynd more closely than any other witness. The Senator pointed out that while the company had used the F.D.A. warning in the insert and in journal advertisements, it had changed the wording in its direct-mail promotion to read:

> Chloromycetin is a potent therapeutic agent and, because certain blood dyscrasias have been associated with its administration, it should not be used indiscriminately or for minor infections. Furthermore, as with certain other drugs, adequate blood studies should be made when the patient requires prolonged or intermittent therapy.

"I am afraid that what you have done here," Kefauver said, "is first to dilute the first part of this warning, which starts off 'Certain blood dyscrasias have been associated,' by putting in front of that 'Chloromycetin is a potent therapeutic agent.' Then you have diluted the blood-study part by saying, 'As with certain other drugs.' You give the impression that certain other drugs have the same requirement. Then you have diluted 'essential' by putting in 'should be.'" He asked why these changes had been made. Loynd's answer was that it was possibly "pride of authorship on the part of one of our medical people."

Shortly after this discussion, Dixon introduced a copy of a memorandum, dated December 15, 1959, from an F.D.A. doctor, Dr. Ralph W. Weilerstein, of San Francisco, describing a visit that two Parke, Davis detail men had paid him ten days earlier in his capacity as a practicing physician. In the course of their talk with him, they had made a number of claims about Chloromycetin, among them that, to quote the doctor, "there is no more danger of blood dyscrasias due to Chloromycetin than there would be from any other antibiotic." In addition, he wrote, "these gentlemen maintained that the above 'facts' were based on figures supplied them by their home office." A few weeks later, the subcommittee learned, Dr. Charles N. Lewis, head of the Antibiotics Branch of the F.D.A.'s Bureau of Medicine, wrote Parke, Davis about this memorandum, saying: "We have had similar complaints from other physicians in recent months about your detail men playing down or minimizing the side effects of this drug. This has [also] occurred at your scientific exhibits at society meetings and elsewhere. The labeling and professional literature for chloramphenicol regularly carry the blood dyscrasia warning which was worked out several years ago, but the net effect is lost if your detail people minimize this important information." Dixon read the reply from an official at Parke, Davis. It said: "I am quite sure

. . . that the statements you report in your letter are not made as a result of any directive from our main office but are in complete contradiction of directions. . . ." More letters and some telephone calls passed between the F.D.A. and the firm, the subcommittee was told, in the course of which Loynd himself declared that if the report was correct he would fire the two men. Dr. Lewis finally asked for copies of the instructions that the company had sent out to its detail men, and, after some delay, Parke, Davis complied.

The first directive, dated March 12, 1952, and signed by Loynd, stated, in part:

> Clinical investigation of the effects of Chloromycetin on body cells and functions is continuing and several additional studies were recently initiated, but, to repeat, up to this date we cannot find any facts that will indicate that Chloromycetin causes aplastic anemia or agranulocytosis.

That was issued before the National Research Council's committee had looked into the matter, Dixon noted. After it had, Parke, Davis sent out another directive, again signed by Loynd, which said:

> Chloromycetin has been officially cleared by the FDA and the National Research Council with *no restrictions* on the number or the range of diseases for which Chloromycetin may be administered.
>
> Thus, Chloromycetin has successfully passed three intensive investigations: originally by Parke, Davis & Co., next by officers of the Food and Drug Administration, then by a special committee of authorities in the fields of hematology and chemotherapy appointed by the National Research Council.

Finally, on September 16, 1952, just a few weeks after the official study of the drug, another letter, from the firm's sales and promotion director, went out to the detail men:

The recent decision reached by the Food and Drug Administration with the assistance of the National Research Council and a board of nationally known medical experts was undoubtedly the highest compliment ever tendered the medical staff of our company.

Kefauver later said that nothing else that emerged in the course of the hearings had made him as indignant as these revelations, yet he remained impassive and soft-spoken. "What impression would be made on a doctor when a detail man told him that the decision was 'undoubtedly the highest compliment ever tendered the medical staff of our company'?" he asked Loynd quietly, and continued, "Everyone knows that you have a great and successful company. You have been in business a long time. Wouldn't the average doctor get the impression that this was just a complete clearance?"

Loynd shook his head vigorously. "Certainly not," he answered. A confused discussion of wording followed, in which Loynd stuck to his guns and Kefauver stuck to his.

In 1961, the sales of Chloromycetin were down again—by more than a fifth. The *Wall Street Journal* reported, "Sales of the drug dropped following publicity over some alleged adverse reactions in patients, and lawsuits involving the product." (During the hearings, Loynd had acknowledged that Parke, Davis had become involved in twenty-five lawsuits over the drug, some of which had been settled out of court while others were pending. Not until March, 1962, did a case come before a jury. It was brought by a California housewife named Carney Love, who charged that her doctor, a co-defendant with Parke, Davis, had given her Chloromycetin for bleeding gums and, later, for bronchitis, with the result that she had come down with aplastic anemia; that this had required the administration of some powerful hormones; and that these had saved her life at the cost of still more side effects. "Now Mrs. Love's face is beet-red and scarred with acne, and she has to shave daily," *Time* magazine reported. "She has muscles like a male athlete's. Doctors warn that because Mrs. Love has a tendency to bleed heavily, she cannot risk a cut or undergo ordinary surgery." The jury awarded her $334,046.)

Loynd took issue with the *Wall Street Journal's* assessment. In an interview published in the Detroit *Free Press,* he attributed a lot of his company's troubles to Senator Kefauver and his drug hearings, which, he said, "caused some very unfavorable publicity, I might say unjustified and some of it ridiculous, which cost us a volume loss on Chloromycetin of about fifteen million dollars." He went on to express the hope that things would quiet down. To an extent, they did. In 1961, the *Physicians' Desk Reference,* a commercially produced manual of therapeutic agents known as "the physician's Bible," carried not the F.D.A.'s warning on Chloromycetin but Parke, Davis's amended version, and in 1962 this was dropped in favor of a statement that the doctor could get information on "dosage, administration, contraindications and precautions" from the package insert, the detail man, or the company. Reports from various parts of the country at the time indicated that many doctors had missed all the furor and were still prescribing Chloromycetin for minor afflictions. In 1962, a travel article in the *Times* listed the medicines that one family had taken along on a trip "at the direction of our family physician"; among them were foot powder, salt tablets, and "forty-eight capsules of Chloromycetin (an antibiotic for dysentery), $24."

IX Kefauver often said—and many members of Congress would agree with him—that government regulatory agencies sooner or later end up partially, or largely, run for, if not by, those whom they are supposed to be regulating. To be sure, these agencies are staffed, for the most part, by diligent, impartial people. But there are exceptions. From the start of his investigation, Kefauver got little coöperation from the F.D.A. and its commissioner, George P. Larrick, who had spoken with pride of his good relations with friends in the industry. It was only by accident that Kefauver found out about Parke, Davis's instructions to its detail men; the F.D.A. had decided to return the directions without making copies of them, or taking any further action, but Mrs. Goodwin had come across them, and had had photostatic copies made before they were sent back to the company. In the hearings themselves, the F.D.A. came in for some harsh criticism, implicit and explicit. The most severe critic was Dr. Barbara Moulton, who appeared before the subcommittee on June 2, 1960, to describe her own experience with the F.D.A. She had worked there as a drug examiner for five years, and then had resigned, she testified, "because the Food and Drug Administration has failed utterly in its solemn task of enforcing those sections of the law dealing with the safety and misbranding of drugs, particularly prescription drugs." The basic trouble, she claimed, was that the drug industry had more influence with the agency than its own medical officers. On one occasion, she went on, she had had grave doubts about the safety of a tranquillizer. "Soon an interview was requested and four representatives of the company appeared," she said, adding that one of her superiors "joined the conference, unexpectedly, as far as I was concerned, and informed the firm that [the] Food and Drug Administration would release the drug without proof of safety for chronic use, and without waiting for completion of the pharmacologic studies." In the case of another tranquillizer, which was already on the market and had been reported to cause addiction, Dr. Moulton said that she had recommended that the agency require the manufacturer to send out a strong warning of this to all physicians. On this occasion, she testified, another of her superiors told her, "'I will not have my policy of friendliness with the industry interfered with.'" Later, she was transferred to a less influential post—as far as drugs went—and when she tried to get reassigned to her old job, the same man refused. His explanation, she said, was that "I was not sufficiently polite to members of the pharmaceutical industry, and one of the large firms had written him requesting that I no longer be permitted to handle their new drug applications." She also said, "I am fully aware that in making this statement I have jeopardized, perhaps irreparably, my own opportunities for future government employment." For well over a year, she found that government jobs were, indeed, closed to her. But, then, in 1961, President Kennedy appointed Dixon chairman of the F.T.C., and Dixon proceeded to hire Dr. Moulton as a medical adviser.

Some months before the drug hearings began, John Lear of the *Saturday Review* also undertook an inquiry into the activities of Dr. Henry Welch, who was then the head of the F.D.A.'s Antibiotics Division and was also the editor-in-chief of two medical journals—*Antibiotics & Chemotherapy* and *Antibiotic Medicine & Clinical Therapy*, both put out by MD Publications, a New York firm, and both relying heavily on pharmaceutical advertising. In January of 1959, Lear went down to Washington to see Welch, and told him point-blank that several doctors claimed he "derived significant income" from his private ventures. As Lear later recounted in the *Saturday Review:*

> "Where my income comes from is my own business," [Welch] said sharply. This, I thought, was a rather extreme view for a man in public office to take. Apparently he had some second thoughts about it himself, for after a pause he added: "I have no financial interest in MD Publications. My only connection is as editor, for which I receive an honorarium. I enjoy editing those journals and I don't intend to give them up." He didn't volunteer the amount of the honorarium or indicate what share of his income it represented. Nor did he mention Medical Encyclopedia, which publishes the proceedings of an annual antibiotics symposium edited by Dr. Welch. I didn't press him for the figures. Conflict of interest, if it exists, is a matter of principle.

As a result of this article, members of Congress addressed a flurry of inquiries to Arthur S. Flemming, Secretary of Health, Education, and Welfare, the F.D.A.'s parent agency. Flemming's office made an investigation, which revealed that Welch had obtained permission from his superiors in 1950 to take on this outside work, and that he had told them, "I may receive yearly honorariums." Within a couple of years, his extra-official activities had become the subject of widespread gossip both in the industry and in medical circles, but no one questioned him officially about the amount of his honorariums until after Lear's article appeared. Then, in February, 1959, John L. Harvey, who was acting F.D.A. director while Larrick, a personal friend of Welch's, was away on sick leave, asked Welch directly how much he was getting. Welch refused to say, and Harvey reported his refusal directly to Flemming. "This started me thinking," Flemming testified in June of 1960, when the subcommittee went into the subject of the drug industry's influence on the government. Apparently, it kept him thinking, for it wasn't until eight months after Harvey's report in October that Flemming directed Dr. Welch to resign from the two journals, and also put out a new memorandum regarding conflict of interest for the enlightenment of the F.D.A. staff. He regarded the moves as merely a precaution, though, and told reporters, "I never heard anyone intimate to me that there was ever any actual conflict of interest."

Among those who came most vigorously to Welch's defense was Loynd. In a personal letter to Flemming, he deplored Lear's "vicious attack on Henry Welch . . . which in my opinion is entirely without foundation," and added, "I do hope that the 'smear' campaign launched by Mr. Lear will not have any effect on the future activities of Henry, since . . . he is making a great contribution to industry as well as Government, all of which is greatly appreciated by those who know him." In the course of Loynd's appearance before the subcommittee, it was brought out that Parke, Davis, acting through its advertising agency, L. W. Frohlich & Co., had sponsored a British edition of *Antibiotic Medicine & Clinical Therapy,* at a cost of $100,000. In a letter marked "Personal and Confidential," Dr. Félix Martí-Ibáñez of New York, owner of MD Publications and co-owner, with Welch, of the Medical Encyclopedia, wrote to Frohlich, "First of all, please allow me to thank you for your kind and most thoughtful help in establishing a liaison between MD

Publications, Inc., and your client, Parke, Davis & Co." The new journal, Martí-Ibáñez went on, "will be of the greatest importance to your client," and he gave several reasons for his statement, among them:

> The editors of the journal hope that good scientific articles with clinical studies on the antibiotics and other Parke, Davis drugs, of sufficient clinical interest and objective value to be accepted, will be submitted for publication.
>
> Parke, Davis & Co. will have first preference in selecting advertising positions in the journal.
>
> The journal will be mailed . . . to 20,000 physicians in England selected from the mailing list submitted by Parke, Davis & Co. as a way to guarantee that the scientific material as well as the advertising of interest to this company will reach preferred physicians on their mailing list.

To get another appraisal of Welch's activities, Kefauver called on Dr. Gideon Nachumi, a resident physician at Kings County Hospital in Brooklyn, who had temporarily interrupted his medical studies in 1956 to work for Pfizer as a medical advertising copywriter. He was there for twelve months, he testified, during which Pfizer was preparing a promotion campaign for Sigmamycin (the drug Lear wrote up later)—a combination of two Pfizer antibiotics that the company claimed had a synergistic effect; that is, the combination was more effective than the components given separately. According to Dr. Nachumi, someone higher up had coined the phrase "a third era in antibiotic therapy" as a basis for the new campaign. "The 'third era' theme . . . has a dramatic quality to it," he explained to the subcommittee. "I think one can see its pictorial value. It kind of implies that the development of Sigmamycin is of comparable importance to the discovery of the broad-spectrum antibiotics [the second era] and perhaps even of penicillin [the first]."

In any event, one of Nachumi's tasks was to edit various papers that were to be delivered at the 1956 International Antibiotics Symposium—an annual event that had been organized four years earlier by Dr. Welch and was co-sponsored by the F.D.A. and the Medical Encyclopedia. To Nachumi's surprise, one of the papers that passed across his desk was a welcoming address written by Dr. Welch himself. He had submitted it for Pfizer's approval, which was granted after Nachumi and his co-workers had dressed it up a bit and added one sentence: "It is quite possible that we are now in a third era of antibiotic therapy: the first being the era of narrow-spectrum antibiotics, penicillin and streptomycin; the second, the era of broad-spectrum therapy; the third being an era of combined therapy where combinations of chemotherapeutic agents, particularly synergistic ones, will be customarily used."

Since Sigmamycin was the only antibiotic combination with supposedly synergistic effects that was being widely promoted at the time, Dr. Nachumi stated, Pfizer considered Dr. Welch's boost to be of great importance. Warren Kiefer, a public-relations man with Pfizer at the time of the symposium, quite agreed. "It isn't very often that this sort of thing happens," he testified, "and for us to have to work with in our campaign what amounted to endorsement by the head of the Antibiotics Division was exceedingly valuable." Another former Pfizer employee, Joseph R. Hixson—he was manager of its domestic pharmaceutical public relations at that period—testified that he had considered the use of the sentence in a press release to be sent out during the symposium unethical and had objected strongly to its inclusion. In fact, he went on, upon learning that it was to be released despite his protest, he called the F.D.A. to see if it had been cleared there, only to find that the F.D.A. seemed quite content with the arrangement. Hixson then told one of his superiors how he felt and what he had done, whereupon he was sharply reprimanded. In the end, the speech was delivered as edited, and was printed in *Antibiotics Annual,* a compendium of the papers delivered at the symposium, which was put out by Medical Encyclopedia. Pfizer bought 260,400 reprints.

On May 5, 1960, Kefauver notified Drs. Welch and Martí-Ibáñez that the hearing relating to them would begin on May 17th. Both of them begged off on medical grounds, the former pleading a heart condition, and the latter glaucoma. Welch's lawyer reported that his client was extremely eager to defend himself, and had said that if his integrity was questioned in any way, "I will want to appear before the committee if you have to carry me in on a stretcher." He never showed up, however—not even when a witness from the General Accounting Office who had gone over subpoenaed records of his financial affairs testified that his honorariums between 1953 and March of 1960 amounted to $287,142.40. Seven days before this was revealed in the hearings, Dr. Welch filed an application for retirement. In accordance with Civil Service regulations, it was granted.

X The most comprehensive presentation of the drug industry's case was made by Dr. Austin Smith, president of the Pharmaceutical Manufacturers Association, who testified for a good part of three days in late February of 1960.

A naturalized citizen of Canadian birth, he was licensed to practice medicine in Ontario but never had, and was not licensed to practice in this country. Prior to becoming head of the P.M.A., however, he had held a number of posts in the A.M.A., most notably the editorship of its *Journal.* As Dr. Smith prepared to deliver his opening statement, he looked up and down the long table before him, and said, "I wonder if any member of the subcommittee knows how much it costs to die." He went on to say that it cost about nine hundred dollars, not including doctors' and lawyers' fees. Then he touched on a personal illness. "The antibiotic that I took I prescribed for myself—four capsules daily for eight days—at a list price of $15.30," he continued. "I thought this was quite an investment for me, and I suppose that this is one time when I could feel that the price of drugs is low." He paused with a surprised look, then added hastily, "In fact, for years I have been speaking of the low cost of drugs." Not only was the cost low, he went on, but people like him, whose lives had been saved, annually contributed an additional billion dollars in taxes to the Treasury.

Dr. Smith later asserted that the drug industry's research costs ran to 9.5 per cent of sales, not 6.3 per cent, as the twenty-two largest manufacturers' own data had shown (Kefauver found this calculation rather mysterious, for although there was no serious disagreement on the numerator [research expenditures], Smith had used a denominator [drug sales] for the entire industry that was twenty-five per cent less than the figures supplied by the twenty-two biggest companies alone). Dr. Smith also said that the industry's profits were far lower than Kefauver maintained (a contention that turned out to have been based not on the F.T.C.

data used by the subcommittee but on a private study that covered only three drug firms).

At one time or another, Dr. Smith made various other assertions, to wit:

"Since 1947 this industry has spent about one billion dollars in research alone."

(A large but meaningless figure, Kefauver pointed out, unless compared to sales and profits.)

"U.S. Department of Labor statistics show the wholesale price of drugs increased only 3 per cent between 1948 and 1958, while the wholesale price index for all industrial products has in the same period risen 22 per cent."

(Kefauver: For one thing, the former percentage was based on only three drugs, none of which typified the situation at hand, and, for another, if a drug manufacturer could stay in business under such conditions, his prices must have been so high to begin with that he didn't have to raise them.)

"There isn't any disease left, to my knowledge, that the pharmaceutical industry is not in some way attempting to attack today."

(Kefauver: Despite the urgency of the struggle to find cures for cancer, research in this field by the industry had been seriously delayed by disputes with the government over patent rights.)

Tackling the by now ragged subject of research, Dr. Smith listed a number of "breakthroughs that are attributable in some significant way to the laboratories of this industry," including "the discovery and development of sulfa drugs," the "discovery and development of the antipsychotic drugs [potent tranquillizers] for treating mental illness," and "the development of the antidiabetics." Dixon challenged each of these claims, pointing out that the first sulfa drug was synthesized in Austria and developed for therapeutic use in Germany, that the antipsychotics were discovered and developed almost entirely in France, England, and Switzerland, and that the principal antidiabetic was discovered and developed in Germany. Dr. Smith stood his ground. Pressed especially hard on the oral antidiabetics, he declared stoutly, "This group of compounds was made available for the physician in the United States through the efforts of the American industry. That is development and making available." He subsequently registered an objection to giving foreigners credit for most of the important drug discoveries. "As a U.S. citizen, I consider this unbecoming, to say the least, of anyone whose security and comfort—yes, even luxuries—stem from the United States of America," he said.

Finally, Dr. Smith strongly defended the use of trade names. Dixon read part of an article that the witness had written for the A.M.A. *Journal* in 1944, in which he had mentioned the "enormous" profits to be made from trade names and had condemned "the absurd practice of prescribing" them when cheaper generic equivalents were available. Kefauver broke in to say, "At that time, you were working for the American Medical Association, and the American Medical Association has been very interested in less expensive drugs so that the doctor can have an interest in the economic welfare of his patient. So, at that time, you recommended generic names. And now you are working for the manufacturers, and you recommend trade names. Does that have anything to do with it?"

"I think, Mr. Chairman, we might make one thing clear right now," Dr. Smith said sharply. "For years, since I have been in professional practice, one type or another, my time and my knowledge have been purchasable, but I never have."

XI In the summer of 1960, just before the last round of investigative hearings was scheduled to begin, Kefauver put aside his duties in the capital to prepare for the Tennessee primary, on August 4th. He appeared to be in serious trouble, for a public-opinion poll had indicated that he was trailing his opponent, Judge Andrew Taylor, by a wide margin. It was thought that Kefauver had been hurt partly by his firm civil-rights stand and partly by his investigation of the drug industry. Pharmaceutical interests had reportedly spent a good bit on Taylor's campaign; they had also got up some literature, which described Kefauver as a Socialist hellbent on ruining the health of the American people, and it was said that doctors and druggists around the state had sent out some eighty thousand pieces of it along with their bills.

On the day that Kefauver left for home, Blair accompanied him from his suite in the Old Senate Office Building to Constitution Avenue, where a car was waiting to take him to National Airport. Even more silent than usual, Kefauver didn't speak until they started down the steps to the street, when he glanced at Blair glumly, and said, "I never should have got mixed up in this drug thing, John. Now I've got the drug people, the pharmacists, and the doctors all stirred up. They're going to throw the book at me down there."

Trying to reassure him, Blair replied that the situation

probably wasn't as serious as it looked from a distance, but Kefauver seemed not to hear him. As they reached the car, the two men shook hands and Blair wished him luck. "You've got nothing to reproach yourself for, Estes," he said. "You did what was right." The Senator stood without moving for a long time, lost in thought. Then, glancing at the Capitol dome across the way, he sighed and got into the car.

One of the most indefatigable campaigners in the history of American politics, Kefauver was also one of the most disorganized. Insisting on seeing everyone who wanted to see him, and a good many who didn't, he invariably fell hours behind schedule, and drove his staff to, and beyond, the point of exhaustion. "Estes wore out nineteen of us a day," Caldwell, his chief aide, said after the 1960 campaign. "He'd get three or four hours' sleep a night and plod on, day in and day out, while the rest of us were stumbling around more dead than alive." A number of Kefauver's colleagues in the Senate were endlessly mystified by his appeal to the voters despite his withdrawn personality and general lack of bonhomie. When Caldwell was asked if the Senator perhaps turned on some red-neck charm when he went back home to campaign, he laughed and shook his head. "Hell, Estes doesn't *have* any charm," he said. "He just comes up to you with that shy, melancholy smile of his and says, 'I'm Estes Kefauver,' and shakes your hand with that huge paw. Suddenly, you feel like you've been wrapped up in a big warm blanket."

At one stop in a medium-sized town during the 1960 campaign, Kefauver announced, to his staff's horrified surprise, that he believed the Negro had as much right as the white man to cast a vote. "The crowd just stared at him and didn't let out a peep," Caldwell recalled afterward.

"When we got on the bus to go on to the next stop, we all shouted and clapped him on the back. We'd never dreamed that he'd do something like that—or that he could possibly get away with it. Later that day, when we returned to the same town, where we planned to spend the night, a big crowd was waiting for us. They screamed and hollered and threw bottles and rocks at the bus. We didn't even slow down."

Throughout the campaign, Kefauver's aides kept urging him to reply to the drug industry's accusations, but he said that it wasn't an important issue, and went on talking in his soft monotone about such matters as N.A.T.O., the U.N., disarmament, Atlantic Union, and other matters that many of his constituents had never heard of. Then, one day toward the close of the campaign, he was giving his more or less standard speech in a small town when the local druggist came out of his store, at the rear of the crowd, and began heckling him. At first, Kefauver ignored the man, but when he persisted, the Senator began citing facts and figures about the high cost of drugs. Suddenly, in a unique display of oratorical fervor, he flung out a long arm with forefinger pointed at the druggist, and cried, "There's one of your enemies!" The audience roared its approval, and there were shouts of "Give it to him, Estes!" From then on, Kefauver made all of his speeches within pointing distance of the local drugstore, and used the same line and gesture, with much the same results. In the end, the pollsters, most of the Tennessee press, the drug industry, and Kefauver himself were astonished when he rolled up a two-to-one victory.

XII Encouraged by this mandate, Kefauver returned to the capital and, after completing the last round of hearings, took the next step in the direction of getting a drug bill passed—namely, by writing one. Three of his primary aims were to lower drug prices; to increase competition to the point where the small manufacturer would get a fair share of the market; and to assure the *emptor* that he needn't *caveat* every time he had a prescription to be filled. "The problem was *how*," Blair said later. "Several million words of claims and counterclaims from the hearings were still dinning in our ears, and we just had too many ideas. Finally, we simply had to sit down in one meeting after another—among ourselves at first, and then, when we had something concrete to propose, with Estes—and try to hammer out from this vast body of material an instrument of control that would be in the public interest." In charge of the actual writing of the bill was Horace L. Flurry, the subcommittee's senior counsel and formerly a trial attorney in the Department of Justice.

In the fall of 1960, Blair made a trip to Europe to give an address before a German economic association, and, on the way back, to find out how some other countries dealt with drug controls. Like just about everyone else, he had always looked upon patents as a sacred part of our economic system—or, indeed, of any capitalistic system—but he soon found out that they were by no means sacrosanct abroad. He observed in a memorandum to Dixon on his return:

At first glance, the idea of limiting the scope of the patent grant might appear to be so extreme as to be not worth serious consideration. Nonetheless, a strong case can be made that in most countries drugs have been recognized as constituting something of a special case, requiring a type of treatment under the patent laws different from that accorded to other products. Indeed, the granting of patents on drug products has been more the exception than the rule. Out of 77 countries for which information is available, only 28 allow product patents on drugs. Behind this attitude has been the moral proposition that no individual or enterprise should profit from human illness and suffering.

He learned, further, that among the major Western powers the United States government alone made no attempt to exert control over drugs, either by limiting patents or by regulating prices. The governments of Switzerland, Italy, and Germany did not permit patents on drug products, and the governments of England and France, which did, had price controls and were empowered by law, if drug prices were judged excessive, to force a manufacturer to grant production rights to others on a royalty basis—a system known as compulsory licensing. In his memorandum, Blair noted that the drug industry in this country was most open to criticism for not lowering prices despite decreases in production costs, and continued, "The simplest method of enabling the consuming public to share in the benefits of technological progress would be to limit the duration of the period of patent protection from the present seventeen to, say, five years." In addition, he suggested that the Sherman Antitrust Act be amended to make it unlawful for drug companies to get together privately to settle disputes over a contested patent. And, finally, he proposed that no modified or combined drugs be considered patentable unless they were proved to be significant improvements over drugs already in use.

All these recommendations were incorporated in the patents section of the bill drafted by the staff, but at a final meeting on that section of the bill, Kefauver decided that he could not go along with the patent cutoff. Although he agreed with Blair that a five-year monopoly would give drug manufacturers ample profits, he felt that a direct threat to the patent system would bring such howls of outrage from the business community at large as to destroy any chance of getting a drug bill passed. After some discussion of alternatives, he came up with a variation on the compulsory-licensing setup used abroad, providing that after three years of exclusive rights the holder of a drug patent would be obliged to license any qualified applicant under a royalty payment of up to eight per cent of sales, which was nearly twice as much as the larger firms ordinarily charged each other when they signed cross-licensing contracts.

Once the patent section of the bill was out of the way, Kefauver and his staff held another series of meetings to consider federal controls over the production, distribution, and promotion of prescription drugs. They devised a scheme whereby the F.D.A. would license all drug manufacturers, who, in order to retain their licenses, would have to meet strict quality-control standards and open their plants periodically to thorough government inspection. This, Kefauver felt, would encourage doctors to prescribe by generic name, would enable patients to save money, and would give small companies a competitive boost. Next, he decided that the Secretary of Health, Education, and Welfare should be given the power to review and revise all current generic names, on the basis of usefulness and simplicity, and to establish all new ones, and that, to help the prescribing physician learn what the generic names were, all labels,

advertisements, and promotional materials containing the trade name of a drug should also display the generic name in the same size type and with equal prominence. He further proposed that advertisements contain explicit warnings about a drug's side effects and a statement of its efficacy; that the Secretary of Health, Education, and Welfare be instructed to publish an annual list of potentially harmful drugs; and that the package insert be sent not to the pharmacist but to the doctor. Then Kefauver recommended an amendment dealing specifically with antibiotics. Under a series of amendments to the Food, Drug, and Cosmetic Act of 1938, as amended, none of the antibiotics that were on the market in 1950—there were only five of them—could be sold until their strength, quality, and purity had been certified by the F.D.A. Between 1950 and 1962, however, dozens of new antibiotics had appeared, so he asked that certification of all antibiotics be made mandatory. Also, while the earlier law had stated that applications to put new drugs on the market would be automatically approved if the F.D.A. failed to act on them within sixty days, Kefauver asked for open-end authority for the F.D.A. by simply canceling the time limit altogether. Finally, he included a provision calling on the manufacturer to prove that every drug he sold was not only safe but effective. As the hearings had shown, the government could do little about ineffective drugs unless they were falsely advertised to the lay public; then it could take the offender to court. Owing to these restrictions, the Senator pointed out, it had taken ten years to ban Hoxey's Cancer Cure—a worthless concoction that sick people spent three to four hundred dollars per treatment for, when they might have been saved by surgery or X-ray therapy.

XIII On April 12, 1961, Senator Kefauver rose in the Senate and submitted the drug bill, which was officially designated S. 1552, for his colleagues' consideration. Among those who considered it were Senators Dirksen, Wiley, and Hruska, for one or another of them attended each of the hearings on the bill—called legislative hearings—which started on July 5th, and ran off and on until the following February. Kefauver had hoped to dispose of that set of hearings expeditiously, but because his Republican opponents had accused him of having been unfair in just about every conceivable way during the earlier hearings, he felt that he must give the drug industry every opportunity to present its case. In the end, the legislative hearings proved to be nearly half as lengthy as the investigative ones, leaving Dirksen and Hruska with only one more accusation—that they had been dragged out unnecessarily.

To a considerable extent, the legislative hearings covered ground that had been gone over earlier. Among the witnesses were representatives of the A.M.A., the P.M.A., the A.F.L.-C.I.O., the United Auto Workers, the National Consumers League, the Justice Department, the Department of Health, Education, and Welfare and the F.D.A., the Patent Office, various health-insurance groups, several organizations of retired people, and quite a number of private physicians. On this occasion, the P.M.A. was represented by Eugene N. Beesley, the president of Lilly and the P.M.A.'s board chairman. Beesley represented the industry's liberal wing and, to Kefauver's delight, he came out for a good part of the bill. However, he drew a sharp and unwavering line where the big money was—in the compulsory-licensing provision. As for the patent section of the bill, it was the subject of an endless dispute that wore out just about everybody, including the industry, which bitterly attacked it, and Kefauver, who patiently defended it.

It was widely reported at the time that the A.M.A. had made an agreement with the P.M.A. to fight the drug bill if the P.M.A. would help defeat the medical-care bill, but, according to an article that appeared in the July 14, 1961, issue of *Science*, the A.M.A. may have had reasons of its own for opposing S. 1552. "It would, if it serves its purposes, sharply reduce the amount of [drug] promotion," the article pointed out, "and this would reduce the A.M.A.'s own resources, since the A.M.A., in fighting the increasingly expensive battle against a government-financed health service, has come to rely heavily on the money its journals earn from drug advertising." In any event, the A.M.A. representatives who appeared before the subcommittee could find nothing whatever in S. 1552 that they approved of. They even opposed the efficacy provision, which just about everyone else, including the P.M.A., the F.D.A., the National Research Council, and even members of the A.M.A.'s own Council on Drugs had supported.

On this point, Dr. Hugh H. Hussey, the A.M.A.'s chairman and principal spokesman at the hearings, argued that only the individual physician could determine the efficacy of a given drug in the treatment of a given patient. A doctor from the Council on Drugs commented, "This argument is a most specious one. The average practicing physician—and I have helped to train hundreds of them—just does not have the time, the facilities, the skill, nor the training to be an expert in the determination of drug efficacy." Moreover, he testified, most doctors believed that the government had already checked drugs for their efficacy. "They may not know the name of the agency," he said, "but they take for granted that there has been some sort of expert and official review preceding the release of the drug for distribution and sale."

Another doctor asserted that the A.M.A. had "euchred itself into this astonishing posture," which, in effect, made "every physician his own Pasteur" and the American people "a willing army of guinea pigs." It was impossible to determine how many drugs were on sale, he added, and referred to "a statement published in *Time* magazine that there were more than 140,000 medicaments available," which he was unable to evaluate "because, on the one hand, [this figure] was published by Dr. Austin Smith in the *Journal* of the American Medical Association when he was its editor, while, on the other hand, it was challenged by Dr. Austin Smith as president of the Pharmaceutical Manufacturers Association and called a libel on the industry."

To throw some light on the A.M.A.'s opposition, Kefauver turned things over to Flurry. Flurry told the subcommittee that in 1957 Dr. George F. Lull, an official of the A.M.A., had spoken at a P.M.A. convention about a breach that had existed in former years between the A.M.A.—especially its Council on Drugs—and the industry. Then Flurry read a portion of Dr. Lull's address:

> We appeared to be a long way from having a common goal or objective of mutual concern in those days. Less than twenty years ago, a considerable portion of the council's time was still devoted to the preparation of reports which were highly critical of many of the drugs then available. . . . [But now] the consideration of advertising has been taken out of the jurisdiction of

the council. Advertising in A.M.A. publications is in the hands of an advertising committee. No consideration of advertising elsewhere is being undertaken. The former official rules of the council have been superseded entirely.

At this point, Kefauver took over and pointed out that in the early fifties the A.M.A. had begun giving up a number of activities that it had been engaged in for some years. Among them were support of a microbiological laboratory to test new drugs, a seal-of-acceptance program (drug advertising in A.M.A. periodicals was limited to products that had been granted the seal), the inspection of drug plants, a measure of control over the choice of generic names, and a campaign for prescribing by generic names. In 1953, Kefauver pointed out, the A.M.A. had had a survey made by a private outfit to determine why its advertising revenue had gone up only three per cent in the past seven years, while that of some other journals had increased by nearly half. According to the survey, seventy-one per cent of the doctors interviewed felt that the seal of acceptance, for instance, was of great value (for over half of them it was more important than a company's good name), but members of the industry had no use for it. Over the next seven years, the A.M.A. had gradually relinquished the policing powers that Kefauver had listed, and in that period its revenue from dues and periodical subscriptions had gone from about five million dollars to almost six, while its advertising income had risen from three and a half million dollars to eight—more than half of the Association's annual earnings from all sources—and the number of advertising pages in the *Journal* had jumped from 470 to 1,402.

"Is it in keeping with human nature that you would be

completely objective when the biggest part of your revenue comes from that source?" Kefauver asked Dr. Hussey.

Dr. Hussey nodded emphatically. "Yes, sir," he said. "It is entirely proper that we should be objective, and we are objective."

Next, Senator Kefauver called on Dr. Irene Till, and she read a notice that had appeared in the *Journal* in 1960: "Every statement that appears in A.M.A. publication ads must be backed by substantiated facts . . . or we won't run it! This is why you can rely on what you read about products that are advertised in the pages of A.M.A. scientific journals." Then Dr. Till produced two advertisements that had appeared in the *Journal* a week apart. The first, for Wyeth Laboratories' Equanil, stated, in part:

> Careful supervision of dose and amount prescribed is advised, especially for patients with a known propensity for taking excessive quantities of drugs. Excessive and prolonged use in susceptible persons (alcoholics, former addicts, and other severe psychoneurotics) has been reported to result in dependence on the drug.

The second, for Carter's Miltown, claimed:

> Simple dosage schedule produces rapid, reliable tranquilization without unpredictable excitation
> No cumulative effects, thus no need for difficult dosage readjustments
> Does not produce depression, Parkinson-like symptoms, jaundice, or agranulocytosis
> Does not impair mental efficiency or normal behavior

Miltown and Equanil, Dr. Till pointed out, were two names for the same drug.

XIV Of the many charges made against the drug industry, one that disturbed Kefauver profoundly was that some pharmaceutical houses seemed to be promoting prescription drugs directly to the layman—sometimes over radio and television but more often in newspapers and magazines. One reason for not advertising such drugs to the patient is that he is not qualified to name his poison—which, of course, all prescription drugs are, in some degree—and another is that doctors resent any interference between them and their patients. The Physicians' Council, a small group of specialists dedicated to improving "the standard of health information disseminated both to the medical profession and the public," has stated in its Code for Advertising that "products which require the special knowledge of a physician for proper administration should not be promoted directly to the public." An extension of this principle is the classic illegibility of doctors' handwriting on prescription blanks, which affords one means of seeing to it that a person doesn't know what medicine he is taking.

Dr. Haskell J. Weinstein, a former medical officer in the clinical-research division of Pfizer, had been the first to accuse the industry of violating this tenet. After remarking, during the investigative hearings, that "there is a rather intense effort to reach [the physician] through the patient," he continued, "It is an unfunny joke in the medical profession that the very latest information on new advances in medicine most often appears in the eminent medical journals such as *Reader's Digest, Time,* and the *Wall Street Journal.* Some of this is legitimate, good reporting. However, much of what appears has in essence been placed by the public-relations staff of the pharmaceutical firms. . . . [They do] not say that the reader should rush to his physician and demand the drug [mentioned], but the implication is usually clear."

Kefauver had thereupon instructed Blair and Mrs. Goodwin to look into the charge, and in time they had presented him with a collection of case examples. Then, early in February of 1962, as the legislative hearings approached their conclusion, Kefauver turned his attention to the activities of the oldest and most specialized public-relations agency in the business—the Medical & Pharmaceutical Information Bureau, a New York outfit headed by John Weilburg, who had formerly been an organizer and negotiator for the Newspaper Guild. In the five years before 1962, M.P.I.B. had represented twenty-three organizations, most of which were drug companies, among them Schering, Merck, Wallace, Bristol, U.S. Vitamin & Pharmaceutical Corp., Chemway Corp., Crookes-Barnes Laboratories, Warner-Lambert Pharmaceutical Corp., Nordson Pharmaceutical Laboratories, Baxter Laboratories, and Warner-Chilcott Laboratories. M.P.I.B., Weilburg testified, served primarily as liaison between these companies and radio, television, and newspaper writers and editors. "In a modest way, the Medical & Pharmaceutical Information Bureau speeds up the process of satisfying the public need for valid information on health and medical subjects," he said, and added, "For ourselves, we take pride in the part we have played in helping to report significant advances in medical science to the public."

On this occasion, Kefauver had as his counsel Bernard Fensterwald, Jr., who had taken over as staff director of the subcommittee after Dixon left, and Mrs. Goodwin. Fensterwald asked Weilburg whether part of M.P.I.B.'s job was not to promote the sale of specific products, and Weilburg replied, "No one has yet shown me that public relations has sold a single prescription drug." At that, Mrs. Goodwin cited one of a number of documents that had been subpoenaed and put into the record, though not all of them came up in the hearings. This one was a letter that M.P.I.B. had sent to Bristol in 1957, outlining the agency's program. Under the heading "General Objectives," the letter included the phrase "to promote the sale of specific products." As Weilburg saw it, this meant nothing more than that promotion of a company was bound to spill over onto its products. In fact, he pointed out, the letter to Bristol had gone on to say as much. It had, but it had also said, "Moreover, narrower and more direct product promotion should also be employed through constant mention of Bristol products in this agency's regular services to news commentators, makeup editors, etc." Of the firm's various techniques, the letter continued, the one that M.P.I.B. felt "would have the broadest and most direct sales promotion results" was a feature called "Spotlight on Health," a newspaper column prepared in mat form ready for printing, which was sent to the editors of two thousand small daily and weekly newspapers across the country.

Kefauver asked, "Isn't this direct sales promotion, Mr. Weilburg?"

Weilburg said he thought not. Rather, he declared, since small papers couldn't afford wire services or syndicated columns, "this is one way of getting medical news to them."

Indeed it was, Kefauver agreed, and pointed out that the medical news involved usually included the trade name of a particular product (he cited Soma, Lenic, and Peritrate, among others) but never the name of the manufacturers (Wallace, Crookes-Barnes, and Warner-Chilcott, respectively), whose general contribution to man's well-being was what M.P.I.B. was supposed to be lauding.

At this point, Fensterwald inquired whether the mats should not have had the word "advertisement" across the top.

Weilburg said he didn't think so, because "you have to pay for advertising space."

Fensterwald smiled. "You seem to have licked that problem," he said. "You seem to get free advertising in two thousand papers."

If the P.M.A. chose not to go as far as the Physicians' Council in limiting drug advertising to the layman, its code of ethics did stipulate that the promotion of new drugs or of new uses of old drugs "prior to adequate clinical acceptance and presentation to the medical profession is not in the best interests of the medical profession or the layman." According to Weilburg's testimony, M.P.I.B. fully subscribed to this. However, several of the subpoenaed documents led Kefauver to wonder how strictly M.P.I.B. had observed it. One of them, a letter that Weilburg himself had written in December, 1960, to Baxter Laboratories, the maker of an anticholestrol preparation trade-named Choloxin, noted that the drug had recently been approved by the Canadian government, and looked forward to the approval of the company's N.D.A., or new drug application, by the F.D.A. Among other things, Weilburg pointed out in this letter that if Canada's acceptance were publicized here, "it may help to speed an N.D.A. clearance," and that "a U.S. story, followed by others based on new clinical work, would help sell Choloxin even before the drug becomes available here." In another document, a letter to Merck about Decadron, its new cortical steroid, M.P.I.B. suggested various ways of promoting the drug before it was cleared by the government, and concluded, "As the above would imply, we feel that the initial effort should be strictly in the news media, saving the consumer magazines for the fall or winter, when Decadron is expected to be past the N.D.A. stage and on the market."

The documents in the record included a series of progess reports from M.P.I.B. to the president of Nordson. One said, in part: "Woman's News Service is distributing a feature-news story on Levonor [a dieting drug] to some 65 newspapers in the United States and Canada," and "NEA Service, Inc., the largest feature syndicate, has accepted a short story on TV snacking and Levonor." Another said that editors of several women's magazines had shied away from any direct endorsement of a drug by name, but added, "We can expect descriptions which will identify the drug to their readers' doctors." A number of writers, the subcommittee learned, had proved to be less reluctant than those editors. Just before Christmas of 1958, M.P.I.B. had prepared a special release on holiday dieting (and Levonor), which it sent to Patricia McCormack, of U.P.I. Later that month, a story under her byline went out to over nine hundred and fifty papers in this country and Canada. A large part of it was taken almost verbatim from the M.P.I.B. release, but here and there Mrs. McCormack put in her own touches:

M.P.I.B.	U.P.I.
To keep calorie control, check with a physician on the use of appetite suppressants. Levonor, a new one, does not stimulate the nervous system and, according to medical reports, can be taken at night to curb pre-dinner hunger without disturbing sleep later on.	To reinforce calorie control, check with a doctor about the use of appetite suppressants. A new one (Levonor) does not stimulate the central nervous system. Medical reports indicate it can be taken at night and does not disturb sleeping later on.

On October 22, 1958, M.P.I.B. sent another progress report to the president of Nordson, in which it referred to "a diet/drug story for *Pageant Magazine,* now being prepared by free-lance writer Donald Cooley, mentioning the use of Levonor," and two months later it reported, further, "Donald Cooley's story on reducing aids has been accepted by *Pageant.*" When Cooley's article appeared in *Pageant,* in May, 1959, it turned out to be an attack on over-the-counter diet drugs. In a box set off from the text, Cooley reminded the reader that "doctor's drugs" (a homely and comforting euphemism for prescription drugs) "are different." One big difference, he explained, was that they "are never advertised to the public." He then went on to name five of them, including Levonor.

"Our releases are written as news stories, and in the style to which our daily press has accustomed us," Weilburg observed in his opening statement. At least one newspaper editor apparently thought that he couldn't possibly improve on a lengthy M.P.I.B. release on Levonor, for it appeared in the *World Telegram* as a news story, with no changes except a new title and no additions except the names of three doctors (taken from another M.P.I.B. release). In his testimony, Weilburg was careful to distinguish between his firm's press releases and its backgrounders; the latter, which were considerably longer, were intended as sources of stories, he said. However, not everyone could tell the difference. Both the *World Telegram* and the New Haven *Sunday Register* printed verbatim an M.P.I.B. backgrounder on vacation medicines, mentioning five of Bristol's drugs.

"Mr. Weilburg," Senator Kefauver said, "this same thing goes on with a number of drugs. You write something about an illness that a lot of people have—for example, one [of the drugs mentioned in a 'Spotlight on Health'] is Peritrate, which will help angina. You have a small 'p.' You don't put it in capitals as a trade name. But when the patient goes to the drugstore to get these [drugs you refer to], he will be told, of course, that these are prescription drugs and he cannot get them. And then the patient will go to the physician and say, 'Well, I have been reading about Peritrate, what a great drug it is,' and attempt to substitute his opinion or convince his doctor, pressure his doctor, to prescribe this because he has been reading something that you wrote, which says it is good for him."

This occurred on the last day but one of the hearings—a day also marked by the vehement behavior of Senator Hruska, who pounded on the table, shouted repeatedly, and dressed down Mrs. Goodwin continuously for her statements. He scoffed at the notion that any physician would give in to a patient's pleas or threats. Weilburg quite agreed. "I cannot imagine any doctor acting that way," he said. At least one of his clients did not share this opinion, it would seem, for a subpoenaed letter to M.P.I.B. from Warner-Chilcott that was put in the record stated, "The question of time seems to me a fairly delicate one. There are two cross patterns to consider. The first, having the material published so patients will go to physicians, and, second, having the physician familiar enough with [the drug] to prescribe it."

A witness who had testified on this point during the investigative hearings was Dr. Perrin H. Long, chairman of the Department of Medicine of the Downstate Medical Center of the State University of New York, who had come to the hearings along with the president of American Cyanamid. Although Dr. Long defended the industry across the board and attacked "those research people, or doctors, who look down their noses at profits" as "fuzzy-minded . . . emotionally disturbed, and jealous," he also assured the subcommittee that some drugs—particularly the sulfas and antibiotics—were widely misused. "By whom?" he asked rhetorically, and answered, "The doctors who prescribed them and by patients who threaten to fire the doctor who doesn't give them their pet antibiotic when they have a common cold, a viral sore throat, a viral pneumonia, or some other type of infection for which treatment with antibiotics is useless." Shortly before the last day ended, Kefauver recalled Dr. Long's statement, and asked an assistant to find it in the voluminous transcript. He then read some more of it to Weilburg and Hruska:

> This happens, gentlemen, far more than you realize. Not long ago, a doctor whom I know was called late one afternoon to see the patient of another doctor who was out of town. She had an acute common cold and also chronic asthma. She imperiously demanded that she be given penicillin, which my friend refused to give her because it is not a good idea to give asthmatics penicillin. The patient got very angry, dismissed the doctor, saying, "I will get a doctor who will do what I say." She did. He gave her an injection of pencillin, and in less than five minutes she died from anaphylactoid reaction produced by the penicillin.

Weilburg remarked merely that he had once tried to persuade his own doctor to give him a certain medicine and had been summarily told to attend to his own business.

"He, of course, knows you did some business with drug companies," Kefauver replied.

In his closing statement, made a couple of minutes later, Kefauver said, "I must say the extent of lay promotion of drugs came as an astonishment to me," and went on to express the hope that some form of his bill would soon be enacted to deal with that and other problems uncovered by the subcommittee. Then, after observing that the hearings had been "a long, hard row," he said he believed that they would produce benefits that would ultimately "accrue to the American people." On that weary note, he adjourned the session at fifteen minutes after eleven on the morning of February 7, 1962, exactly twenty-six months and 12,885 pages of testimony after the opening day, and the hearings officially came to an end.

Part Three. THE BILL

I To many lawmakers on Capitol Hill nothing is more unsettling than the prospect of making a law—at any rate, a law involving the least trace of controversy. The passage of almost any piece of legislation is bound to offend someone, and in politics it is not so much the good will of one's friends that counts as the wrath of one's enemies. The members of Congress who have laid down its parliamentary rules over the years appear to have been well aware of the advantages of legislative stalemate. In fact, as Professor Daniel M. Berman, a political scientist at American University, in Washington, has written, "The procedures that follow the introduction of a bill and its reference to committee are so formidable that they might well have been devised by men who hated the thought that legislation would ever be enacted." It often happens that the strongest opponent of new legislation is a special-interest group, such as business, labor, the farmers, or the professions—a group of the sort that James Madison described in *The Federalist Papers* as being "actuated by some common impulse of passion, or of interest, adverse to the right of other citizens, or to the permanent and aggregate interests of the community." Yet if many politicians ignore the community's interests much of the time, all politicians know that to ignore them altogether will sooner or later mean answering for it at the polls. Accordingly, for a conservative legislator with a sizable bloc of liberal constituents the most prudent course may be to praise a progressive measure both on the floor and in speeches back home, and then, in the privacy of an executive-committee meeting, to vote against it, or at least to pierce it with a few loopholes, while a liberal with a good many conservative constituents may find it prudent to reverse the strategy.

An even simpler strategy for someone who is working both sides of the street is to see to it that the committee involved doesn't meet at all. Representative (more commonly known as Judge) Howard W. Smith, the conservative chairman of the House Rules Committee, which controls all measures submitted to the lower body, remarked not long ago, "Some folks might be surprised to know the number of people from both sides of the aisle who have, under deep stress about bills, come to me and said, 'Judge, we wish you'd take another vacation. We'll get up a pot and pay for it.' This year, everybody, I think, that came to see me wanted to help paint my barn or something like that."

Now and then, the sponsor of a controversial public-interest bill can overcome routine political hypocrisy of this sort. But he must be backed first by the people and ultimately by the administration. As Professor Berman noted, "Only with the firm support of a President, particularly in his role as party leader, can there ever be a favorable prognosis for liberal legislation in Congress." In the last generation, undoubtedly the most striking example of the kind of skill and tenacity it takes to put through a progressive, and controversial, bill was the battle waged by the late Senator George W. Norris, of Nebraska, an independent Republican, to set up the Tennessee Valley Authority. For twelve years, starting in 1921, he fought for the project against the opposion of three presidents, several powerful colleagues, many powerful lobbyists, and the first Henry Ford (who had his own realty scheme for the area), and then, in 1933, after the election of Franklin D. Roosevelt, he won.

Senator Kefauver had been born and raised in the Tennessee Valley, and he had seen what Norris's project had accomplished for that impoverished region. Along the way, he had become a great admirer of Norris, and in many ways was just as skillful a politician and certainly as tenacious a one. By the winter of 1962, Kefauver felt that he was in even a stronger position than the Norris of 1933. To be sure, his goal of getting a drug law enacted scarcely compared, either in its scope or controversial nature, to the T.V.A.; moreover, he had fewer opponents and far wider support. At the time, he believed that he had the backing of both the public and the administration. In his twenty-three years in Congress, he had never received anything approaching the numbers of letters that reached his desk congratulating him on his drug investigation and hearings. As for the administration, President Kennedy had said in his 1962 State of the Union Message, "To protect our consumers from the careless and the unscrupulous, I shall recommend improvements in the food and drug laws." Then he had gone on to call for a federal program for medical care for the aged, which, Kefauver felt, would obviously be far less costly to the taxpayer if drugs were cheaper, since the price of medicine was one of the largest items in the elderly person's budget. Moreover, Kennedy was about to issue a Consumer Message—the first to come out of the White House since 1906, when Theodore Roosevelt signed the original Pure Food and Drug Act—and it was rumored that the Message would press some of the 1960 Democratic platform promises, one of which was to do something about "flagrant profiteering" in the drug industry. Finally, though Kennedy and Kefauver had fought bitterly for the 1956 Vice-Presidential nomination, Kefauver had gone on to campaign for Kennedy in 1960 in thirty states—more than any other Senator. So far, all he had got in return was the opportunity to suggest Dixon for chairman of the F.T.C.

After the legislative hearings, a number of Kefauver's critics within the government—principally in H.E.W.—charged that S. 1552 was rather loosely put together, so Kefauver and his staff tightened the language, rewrote some portions, and added others that had been recommended in the hearings on the bill. For one thing, the Sherman Antitrust Act amendment was changed from making it unlawful for drug firms to enter into licensing agreements while a patent was pending to requiring them to file all such agreements with the Commissioner of Patents and the F.T.C. so that they would be available as evidence in antitrust cases. With a few other minor changes, Kefauver resubmitted the bill, under the same number, to the Senate on March 4, 1962.

II

For the most part, the drug industry dealt with the threat of restrictive legislation through the Pharmaceutical Manufacturers Association, which represented a hundred and forty drug companies—companies that accounted for more than nine-tenths of the nation's drug business. The

P.M.A. had a divided reaction to Kefauver's first bill, according to a lobbyist who participated in the industry's deliberations. There was a hard-line group that wanted to sweep into Washington and try to buy up the necessary votes, and there was a more liberal group opposed to such statehouse tactics, which was led by the heads of two of the most reputable concerns in the field—John T. Connor, of Merck, and Eugene N. Beesley, of Lilly. As chairman of the P.M.A., Beesley naturally had a good deal of influence. Like Merck, Lilly had long been observing many of the rules that Kefauver hoped to establish formally, and it had nevertheless been making a profit of over thirteen per cent on its sales. Lilly's scientists, it appears, had become uneasy about the practices of some other drug companies, and they strongly urged Beesley to support a good part of the proposed legislation. Lilly's public-relations men were of the same mind, if for somewhat less elevated reasons. The Kefauver hearings had all but indelibly besmirched the pharmaceutical business, they felt, and they held that the best countermeasure would be to encourage a certain amount of remedial legislation. Perhaps their most compelling argument was that history had shown drug legislation to have a way of getting stronger the longer it lay around Capitol Hill, so the chances were that if the companies succeeded in blocking Kefauver's bill, they would sooner or later get something worse. The proponents of this view—backed up by Edward H. Foley, a former New Dealer who was serving as the P.M.A.'s legislative strategist, and Lloyd N. Cutler, the P.M.A.'s special counsel—finally prevailed. However, there was no disagreement at all about the compulsory-licensing provision (the bill's price-cutting amendment), and, to a lesser extent, the amendment requiring that all advertising and promotion describe the bad as well as the good effects of a drug. Both of these, one of the industry's leaders said, "we mean to fight to the death."

At the start, it was a gentlemen's war by and large, although the right-wingers in the industry did at times resort to guerrilla tactics. Some sent doctors lavish, and distorted, brochures urging them to write to their senators and representatives about the vicious attack that Kefauver was making on the free-enterprise system, and assuring them that his bill would wipe out the industry's ability to engage in research. Others got their employees to send letters to the key men on the subcommittee; a perusal of Senator Hart's mail, for instance, revealed scores of letters from constituents in Detroit—most of them identical. In addition, some drug firms set up training programs for several thousand detail men, designed to prepare them to give lectures around the country before audiences of P.-T.A. groups, women's clubs, and fraternal organizations on the dire consequences to the health of the American people if the Kefauver bill became law.

Meanwhile, Kefauver was lining up support for his bill. Up to the time that he filed the amended version, he had held off from approaching the President for an outright endorsement. For one thing, he knew that his compulsory-licensing provision would undoubtedly be attacked by the business world at large as an attempt to destroy our patent system. For another, he was well aware that although the consumer accounts for two-thirds of all the spending in the economy, he has no lobby of any weight to work on his behalf behind the scenes, and that, as a result, nothing is more difficult than getting a consumer-protection bill through Congress. And, for a third, he feared that the indifferent or even hostile reactions of the various executive agencies he had asked for help during his investigation might have penetrated to the White House, for even the most independent administration is greatly influenced by the entrenched civil servants under it, whom it must turn to for expert advice when a decision affecting their jurisdiction has to be made. Their advice is not always impartial. As Judge Lee Loevinger, head of the Antitrust Division of the Department of Justice at the time of the drug hearings, has pointed out, a good many civil servants fail to qualify as public servants. "Unfortunately, the history of every regulatory agency in the government is that it comes to represent the industry or groups it's supposed to control," he said recently. "All of these agencies were fine when they were first set up, but before long they became infiltrated by the regulatees and are now more or less run by and for them. It's not a question of venality, either. More, the agency people consort with this or that representative of some special-interest group, and finally they all come to think alike. Every company that's concerned about government control and is big enough to manage it hires a man—or maybe four or five men—at anywhere from thirty to seventy thousand dollars a year to find out what we're up to. And, by God, they find out! They wine and dine agency people and get to be great friends with them. Like a lot of people without much money, some bureaucrats are impressed by being around big shots and by the big life. Sooner or later, all of these agencies end up with constituents. And they represent them damned well, too."

In any event, upon learning, early in March of 1962, that President Kennedy was going to issue his Consumer Message within a couple of weeks, Kefauver decided to make his pitch. On the evening of March 7th, accompanied by three of the top-ranking members of his personal and subcommittee staffs—Caldwell, Fensterwald, and Blair—the Senator left his suite of offices and went to the White House for a conference with Myer Feldman, the President's deputy special counsel and one of his overseers of legislative matters. "I told Kefauver that I'd like his views on the Consumer Message," Feldman said afterward. "He gave them to me, and we incorporated some of them." Kefauver's primary suggestion was that the Message include a direct endorsement of S. 1552, but he also asked the administration to refrain from sending a drug bill of its own to Congress along with the Message, since that would necessitate further hearings, which might prevent passage of any bill that session. Feldman promised to pass both requests on to the President.

Kefauver had been hoping for a decision—at least on the question of endorsement—that same night, for the subcommittee was scheduled to meet the following morning to vote on S. 1552, and he was by no means certain of the outcome. Although he could count on the support of the four other Democratic members—Carroll, Long, Hart, and Dodd—the latter two were out of town, leaving him with a three-to-three deadlock with the Republicans if not only Dirksen and Hruska but also Wiley turned up. By ten-thirty next morning, when the subcommittee was scheduled to convene in Dirksen's office, Kefauver had received no word from the White House, so he set out for the meeting, accompanied by Blair and Caldwell. Dirksen, Hruska, and Long were there when he arrived, making it a two-to-two, instead of a three-to-three, standoff. (Wiley, who was up for reëlection that year, had decided to play it safe and sit things out—in the Senate chamber down the hall.) Kefauver sat down and slowly began shuffling through his papers, in the hope that Carroll would turn up before he was forced to call for a vote.

After a few minutes, Dirksen smiled and said, "Shall we proceed, Mr. Chairman?"

Caldwell got up, hurried out to a telephone, and called Carroll's administrative assistant, Harry Schnibbe. "For God's sake, get John over here!" he cried. "We're lost without him."

When Caldwell returned to the office, he found Kefauver still playing for time. Five minutes later, when he had just about exhausted all possible devices for delay, the door flew open and Carroll burst in. Now it was Kefauver's turn to smile. "All right, gentlemen, shall we proceed?" he asked crisply. On amendment after amendment, the votes clicked off along party lines, and S. 1552 was reported out unaltered.

III Although Kefauver naturally was gratified, he was hardly confident about getting the bill over the second hurdle with quite the same ease. "It next goes to the parent Senate Judiciary Committee, where its future is clouded," the *Wall Street Journal* noted, and went on to say, "The full committee is conservative-tinged and seldom sees eye-to-eye with its antitrust subcommittee." The chairman of the full committee was Senator James O. Eastland, of Mississippi, and it had six members besides the eight on the subcommittee, three of them conservative Southern Democrats (Olin D. Johnston, of South Carolina; John L. McClellan, of Arkansas; and Sam J. Ervin, Jr., of North Carolina), and three conservative-to-moderate Republicans (Hugh Scott, of Pennsylvania; Hiram L. Fong, of Hawaii; and Kenneth B. Keating, of New York). Kefauver could scarcely hope that the majority of the committee would see eye to eye with the subcommittee unless the President spoke out for S. 1552. As he saw it, the Southern Democrats ordinarily followed the Party leadership when they didn't feel that a matter of principle was at stake. Moreover, if the administration were to make a popular issue of drugs, a Republican or two could be counted on to join in.

On March 15th, a week after the subcommittee reported the bill out, President Kennedy released the text of his Consumer Message, which deeply disappointed Kefauver. While the administration did not send Congress its own drug bill, little else that the Senator had asked for had been granted. The Message recommended several of Kefauver's amendments (though none of the ones dealing with prices), but it did so without attributing them to Kefauver, and it said nothing whatever about S. 1552.

That afternoon, Kefauver telephoned Feldman and said he was especially upset by the fact that the Message had contained nothing about cutting drug prices, and that he intended to put out a press release saying as much. Feldman assured him that the administration stood behind the principles embodied in S. 1552 all the way. "I wish to hell you'd made that clear in the Message," Kefauver said, and hung up.

"Estes is disliked in a lot of quarters because he's such a lone wolf—and, what's worse, a reformer," one very high administration official later explained. "And the White House is no exception. I don't know who it is there that doesn't care for him, but somebody certainly doesn't. Besides that, the President simply isn't very interested in domestic matters, and never has been. Some of us have urged him again and again to take on these tough domestic issues, but he's been very ambivalent about them. He doesn't want to get involved in anything controversial, and just about everything that Kefauver puts his hand to is controversial."

On the Hill, the general view was that the Consumer Message was anything but controversial—or original. "Most of the proposals endorsed have been gathering lichen on Capitol Hill," the Washington *Post* observed in an editorial on the Message. A good many liberals in Congress were irritated not just by the attempt to take credit for proposals originating elsewhere, but by the administration's over-all approach to dealing with the consumer's lack of national representation. In the 1960 campaign, Senator Kennedy had called for "a consumer counsel, backed by a suitable staff, to speak for consumers in formulation of government policies and to represent consumers in administrative proceedings." Kefauver and a number of other senators had gone further and filed a bill to create a Department of Consumers, at the cabinet level. However, the Message proposed, instead of either measure, a Consumer Council, an advisory body without executive power, which was to be subordinated to the Council of Economic Advisers. The New York *Times*, in an editorial on the subject, dismissed the proposal as "a bone for the consumer."

In any case, the morning after the Message was released, the Judiciary Committee met, and right after Eastland had called the meeting to order, Dirksen moved that S. 1552 be referred to Senator McClellan's Subcommittee on Patents and Trademarks for further consideration. Kefauver objected strongly. "This is an obvious attempt to kill the measure," he said, and went on to point out that when he originally filed the bill, McClellan had agreed to let him handle the whole thing, including the patent provisions. Moreover, he added, the subject had been fully aired during the hearings. McClellan acknowledged that he had made such an agreement, but said he now believed that the patent provisions needed further study after all. Then Dirksen took the floor to argue that whenever a bill reported out by one subcommittee covered material that another subcommittee traditionally had jurisdiction over, the latter had both a right and a duty to examine it. As Dirksen spoke, Kefauver looked around the table and realized that he had lost. "I figured they'd win if they made such a motion," he said afterward. "First of all, the administration's failure to support me left the committee members free to vote as they pleased. Some of them were opposed to *any* bill, some respected the jurisdictional rights of McClellan's subcommittee, and some were glad to have an excuse not to have to take sides. The jurisdiction issue got them all off the hook." He had not anticipated how badly he would be defeated, however. Only Senator Hart, who was co-sponsor of the bill and his staunchest ally on the committee, voted with him.

When Kefauver emerged from the conference, he paused just long enough to give the reporters on hand a curt account of what had taken place, and then he walked down the hall alone—a tall, heavy figure with a slightly rolling gait. McClellan assured the reporters that he had not sought jurisdiction over the bill merely to kill it. "I know some others who want to, though," he added. As for Dirksen, he came out of the conference room with what one trade paper called "a victory smile." He had good reason to be pleased. According to the Pink Sheet, the vote had "killed any chance of Senate approval of the drug bill this year."

Leaks to the press about executive sessions, which some senators deplore, are certainly no more common than leaks to special-interest representatives, who often learn who did what at such meetings within minutes of their conclusion. In fact, it would appear that some committee decisions are revealed even before they are made. The day that the Judiciary Committee voted to send S. 1552 to McClellan's subcommittee, the Washington *Post* listed the previous day's stock-market quotations under the headline "MIXED MART TURNS HIGHER ON LATE RALLY. DRUGS, STEELS LEAD RISE." One senator, a man experienced in such matters, attributed the market rise to a leak. "That's exactly the way it happens," he said.

Despite the Pink Sheet's appraisal, Kefauver had by no means given up hope of getting S. 1552 passed that session, although he agreed that it would be practically impossible to get it through in anything resembling its original form, for his opponents clearly had control over the Judiciary Committee on this issue. "All you ordinarily need to swing a committee one way or another is two or three votes," a lobbyist for the drug industry remarked later. "Well, we were able to persuade Eastland, McClellan, Johnston, and Ervin to go along. I must say we didn't have much trouble talking them into it. They all dislike Kefauver for his liberalism—mostly because he refused to sign the Southern Manifesto. But Eastland didn't need any persuading at all. He just can't stand Estes Kefauver."

According to a column by Drew Pearson that appeared a couple of weeks later, some of the credit was Dirksen's, for he had talked McClellan into reversing himself. "One of the biggest contributors to the Republican Party is Spencer Olin of the Olin Mathieson combine, sole owners of Squibb . . .

[who] was long financial chairman of the Republican National Committee and a generous contributor to Dirksen's election," Pearson wrote. Continuing, he listed the contributions that several officers of Olin Mathieson had made to the G.O.P. in 1956, the last year for which figures were available; the total came to a little over a hundred thousand dollars. Then, on April 2nd, in a column entitled "President Skips Drug Prices," Pearson wrote that the White House staff had advised President Kennedy to sidestep the drug bill, because the compulsory-licensing provision was too controversial. Sooner or later, however, the administration would face a showdown on the drug issue, Pearson declared. "A few discreet phone calls from the White House unquestionably could now push the drug bill through the Senate," he added. Extremely sensitive to adverse comment of this sort, the White House, in the person of Feldman, did make some phone calls—to Blair and to H.E.W.—and Kefauver was assured that the President would write to Eastland urging action on S. 1552.

Early in April, McClellan rounded up the members of his subcommittee—Kefauver, Johnston, Hart, Wiley, and Scott—for several meetings to consider the bill's patent sections. Then, on April 9th, he moved that the subcommittee vote on the bill. Those who had suspected that he meant to delay matters indefinitely were bewildered by this action, but the vote itself made everything clear; by a vote of four-to-two, with Kefauver and Hart opposed, the bill was sent back to the full committee shorn of its compulsory-licensing and Sherman Act amendments. Kefauver declared that he would reintroduce the excluded amendments when the bill got to the floor, but it was generally thought that this would be futile, since both the administration and the full committee had repudiated them. Once these provisions were excised, the drug industry heaved a collective sigh of relief; the greater part of its goal had been achieved, and all that remained was to whittle down some of the more corrosive edges of the bill—such as the advertising amendment—in subsequent meetings of the full committee.

The day after the vote in McClellan's subcommittee, the President sent his letter to Eastland. Though Kefauver was dismayed at the timing and at certain omissions, he was pleased by a couple of new provisions that the letter recommended—a requirement that drug manufacturers keep records of adverse reactions to the use of their products, for the government's perusal, and an amendment giving H.E.W. the power to withdraw approval of a drug "on the basis of a substantial doubt of its efficacy, or safety." The letter concluded, "With the above changes, S. 1552 adequately deals with the most pressing problems in the drug field, and it is my sincere wish that it be enacted during the current session of the Congress."

On Capitol Hill, the most widely held explanation for the administration's sudden interest in the Kefauver bill was that the President had become increasingly concerned about the sluggish progress of his legislative program. By this time, it was generally believed that the Medicare plan had almost no chance of getting through both houses that session. Moreover, the A.F.L.-C.I.O. and a number of other unions, which had strongly supported S. 1552 from the start, were beginning to grumble about his apparent disinterest in the measure. Now, since the drug industry no longer opposed it so adamantly, the administration, it was commonly said, had everything to gain and nothing to lose.

IV If, as one senator has said, confusion is the clearest thing about the government, probably the most compelling thing, for good or ill, is accident. The day after the President's letter reached Eastland, Blair was studying a copy of it in his office when his secretary, a vivacious Tennessean by the name of Jo Anne Youngblood, hurried in with that morning's New York *Times* and showed him an article about a speech that Dr. Helen B. Taussig, a professor of pediatrics at Johns Hopkins and co-developer of the blue-baby operation, had delivered before a Philadelphia meeting of the American College of Physicians. In her speech, Dr. Taussig reported that the widespread use by women during early pregnancy of a presumably harmless sleeping pill, generically known as thalidomide, had resulted in the birth of between thirty-five hundred and five thousand hopelessly deformed babies. (Subsequent figures raised the estimate to more than seven thousand.) Most of the cases had occurred in West Germany, where thalidomide was first marketed, but some had been scattered around the globe. "This compound could have passed our drug laws," Dr. Taussig told her audience. "There is no question but what we must strengthen our food-and-drug regulations." She went on to say that the only reason thalidomide had not been sold here was that the Wm. S. Merrell Company, a hundred-and-thirty-four-year-old pharmaceutical house in Cincinnati that was its American licensee, had submitted what the F.D.A. considered insufficient data in its application to market the drug. As soon as Blair had read the story, he called in Mrs. Wendt, the subcommittee's triple-threat lawyer, bacteriologist, and chemist, and asked her to see what she could find out about thalidomide.

On April 23rd, the administration came up with another legislative surprise for the Kefauver forces: It sent a drug bill of its own to Capitol Hill. Technically, Kefauver's earlier request was honored, for the President sent the measure only to the House—by way of Representative Oren Harris, of Arkansas, the chairman of the Interstate and Foreign Commerce Committee. As Kefauver saw it, the Harris bill, as it came to be called, was generally much weaker than his bill (at least, before S. 1552 was shorn of its compulsory-licensing provision), largely because it contained no patent provisions or anything else to help lower drug prices. Whatever the relative merits of the two bills, the administration's would clearly never have existed without the background of the drug hearings, for, in large part, it was based on what they had revealed.

Feldman was quick to justify the administration's move. "We're backing Senator Kefauver," he said. "In the Senate we're using his bill as our vehicle, and in the House the Harris bill."

According to the Pink Sheet, the President's letter to Eastland had "imposed a close limitation on the amount of material that H.E.W. and F.D.A. could impose. This has created a neat problem of legislative maneuvering in Congressional strategy for H.E.W. Everybody concerned with drug controls, in fact, was cooking up some sort of legislative strategy last week, and the atmosphere in Washington drug circles was heavy with secret intrigues."

One reporter, who got the impression that H.E.W. was not entirely antagonistic to the industry's hopes for a mild bill, asked Feldman what would happen if H.E.W. tried to push through a pro-industry measure. Feldman shook his head sharply. "I can assure you that if H.E.W. tries to go outside the President's orders, I'll stop it," he said, thereby conceding that H.E.W. was quite capable of trying. "Any changes made will be examined by me, and I will clear them with Kefauver, just as I did the Harris bill, which he approved."

Kefauver was puzzled by the remark. "I don't recall that Feldman cleared anything with me," he said. "About all that he told me was that they were sending a bill covering F.D.A. stuff to Harris. He didn't tell me what was in it. I was disappointed by their move. It makes it a lot more difficult to get a good bill passed, because when Senate and House bills are different, you're likely to end up with the weakest parts of both. Besides, if the administration is truly supporting me, as he claims, why introduce another bill in the House? Why not use Celler's companion measure?"

That same day, Kefauver got some more disheartening news: McClellan had not sent S. 1552 back to the Judiciary Committee, but still had it in his office. Upon learning this, Kefauver phoned McClellan, and received his promise that the bill would be returned at once. Kefauver was gratified by getting this much action, but one of the attorneys on his staff was of the opinion that he was holding onto hope more than reality. "McClellan stalled just long enough to give the administration a chance to say, 'Well, S. 1552 is stuck, so we've got to get something else moving,'" he said. "Then they submit a bill that the industry helped write and therefore doesn't really object to. In the end, they get full credit, without actually doing much to protect the public. If you ask me, we've had it."

Feldman disagreed. "I think the Kefauver bill's chances are very good," he said the following day. "I'm reasonably sure that we'll get it on the Senate calendar soon and passed substantially as it stands this session." He seemed to be about the only person in Washington who thought so.

V Although the Harris bill was designed to supersede the Celler bill, the latter was far from dead, and Kefauver prevailed upon Celler to stir up matters by going ahead with some further drug hearings. Celler, who is known as a faithful party man, was able to justify his alliance with Kefauver by assuming that the President's letter to Eastland meant what it said when it asked for action on the Kefauver drug bill. The Celler hearings, which began on May 17th, occupied only four days and involved only twenty-one witnesses—two-thirds of them speaking on behalf of the drug industry—but in some ways they were more trenchant than those conducted by Kefauver. Of course, Celler had the advantage of being able to use the earlier hearings as a base, but, more important, he was far less concerned about the usual charges in such a case of being a publicity hunter. As he saw it, the industry had been accused of being greedy and negligent, and now it was simply a question of seeing whether the indictment would stick. Moreover, Celler's peppery, no-nonsense manner, in contrast to Kefauver's soft-spoken patience and deference, often put witnesses off their feed before they sat down at the witness table.

The difference in style and approach was nowhere more clear than in the way the two men handled the most eminent witness to appear before them—Dr. Vannevar Bush, director of the Office of Scientific Research and Development during the Second World War, vice-president of MIT, president of the Carnegie Institution of Washington, and, until he retired between the two sets of hearings, chairman of the board of Merck. At the Kefauver hearings, Dr. Bush consistently met with fairly gentle treatment, and upon the conclusion of his testimony the audience, which was made up almost entirely of industry people, rose to its feet and broke into wild applause. Celler was less deeply impressed than Kefauver by the witness's age and career, possibly because he himself was older than Bush and had been a member of Congress for forty years. At both hearings, Bush praised the industry at some length, and attacked all government attempts to regulate it further. During the House hearings, however, Celler eventually broke in. "Don't try to be an apologist for everything," he said gruffly. "I am afraid your whole testimony has been one grand, great, big apology, and it does not sit well, Dr. Bush. It really does not. You are too honest a man for that."

On the key point brought up during the Celler hearings, Bush was too honest for some of the industry people in the audience. "Is it your belief that in the realm of patented drugs the competition has tended to take the form of price competition?" he was asked.

"No, sir, I do not," Bush answered. "I think it has mostly taken the form of quality competition."

On one occasion in the Celler hearings, it appeared that the administration was fighting not only Kefauver but itself. At least, that was the impression conveyed by two of the witnesses it sent over to testify—David L. Ladd, head of the Patent Office, who came out against the compulsory-licensing provision, and Judge Loevinger, of the Justice Department's Antitrust Division, who came out for it. "I heard, just before the hearings, what Loevinger was going to do, and I simply didn't believe it," one administration official later confessed. He was not the only one in the executive branch who was surprised. When Loevinger informed the Budget Bureau, which serves as the President's watchdog over all pending legislation, about his intentions, he was reprimanded for taking a public stand on a matter that the administration was undecided about. "We said we had taken this position for the Department before," Loevinger said afterward, "and would emphasize that it was just the department's view and not the administration's. Finally, they said okay."

Kefauver was greatly encouraged by this turn, for, as the Pink Sheet noted at the time, "Celler's brief hearings thus take on far greater importance than might otherwise have been anticipated. . . . Getting the Attorney-General's views out on the public record might be enough to swing powerful—and power conscious—officials in other interested agencies into the same line."

One of the few witnesses to appear before the Celler committee who endorsed the bill—that is, the non-patent part of it—was Dr. M. Harold Book, director of laboratories at the Norristown State Hospital, in Pennsylvania, and assistant professor of neuropathology at the University of Pennsylvania's Graduate School of Medicine. On hand to testify principally about the growing medical problem presented by the side effects of drugs, Dr. Book pointed out that in recent months a number of manufacturers had taken several once highly praised drugs off the market. "These incidents suggest that the preliminary testing was hasty and faulty," he stated. After describing some of the side effects involved, he went on, "In my long experience as a pathologist, I have performed some two thousand autopsies in several hospitals. In the last eight or nine years, I, and many other pathologists, have noticed a distinct increase in the number of serious adverse effects, even deaths, resulting from the widespread use of many of the newer so-called wonder drugs. . . . Many of these unusual effects of drugs . . . are only uncovered at [the time of] autopsy. Unfortunately, postmortems are done in only a small percentage of deaths in this country, so that much of this badly needed information goes to the grave with the patient."

By all odds, the most appalling examples in history of side effects from drugs were among those who survived, as graphically demonstrated by another witness—Dr. Taussig, who had been contacted by Celler's staff after her speech in Philadelphia about the malforming effects of thalidomide. She told of going to West Germany earlier in the year to study the epidemic of babies who were afflicted with a theretofore rare malady known as phocomelia—from the Greek words "*phoko*" and "*melos*," meaning "seal" and "limb." After describing the physical effects of thalidomide and remarking that few of the infants crippled by it also suffered mental damage, Dr. Taussig projected slides to show what the children looked like.

When Dr. Taussig had finished, Representative Peter W. Rodino, Jr., of New Jersey, asked, "You say, Doctor, that . . . the children are born with a normal mentality?'

Dr. Taussig replied that ninety-nine out of a hundred of them were, and went on, "Let me assure you, there is nothing you see in the pictures that is as terrible as seeing the children. Most of these children, of course, have been born within the last year and are not walking around. But [I realized] that they were going to be unable to dress themselves, unable to feed themselves, unable to bathe themselves without a great deal of help. Bathe and dress they certainly cannot. Prosthesis will help, but if they have no arms or legs, it looks pretty hopeless."

To the astonishment of those who attended the hearings, not a word about Dr. Taussig's testimony appeared in the newspapers. There were some dark mutterings about a press blackout, but actually nothing so sinister had occurred. It was simply that Celler's staff had not announced that a witness was about to say something important. Several weeks later, when the thalidomide story suddenly hit the front pages of every newspaper in the country, a wire-service reporter assigned to the Hill complained about the failure of Celler's staff to alert him to Dr. Taussig's appearance. "I don't know what's wrong with those guys over there," he said. "The biggest story of the year, and they just sat on it."

Blair, for one, was not displeased by the news gap. "I tried to talk Celler's people out of using Dr. Taussig," he explained at the time. "It's too early to spring this kind of story. All the various bills are still far from reaching the floor of either house, and it's clear that the thalidomide story, or something like it, is just what we need to ram through some legislation. In a situation like this, timing is vital."

VI

Compromise is like rain—too much of it too soon, and the crop washes away. As the congressional session progressed, there were increasingly loud complaints from Democrats in both houses about the administration's haste to barter. "In some cases, administration lobbying has been inept," Karl E. Meyer, a Washington *Post* editorial writer, observed in an article that appeared in the *New Statesman*. "In others, according to qualified observers, the White House has followed what has been called 'a policy of anticipatory surrender,' as in federal aid to education and Medicare. 'These matters are often delegated to mechanics who wind up asking for little and getting nothing,' remarks someone close to the cockpit. 'It is a case of the uncommitted haggling with the uncommitted.' "

Toward the end of May, it became clear that despite the President's letter to Eastland, the administration was not eager to tangle with the opponents of the Kefauver drug bill, for Congressman Harris announced that he intended to begin holding hearings on *his* bill on June 19th. This played directly into the hands of those opposed to S. 1552, for Harris's committee had no Kefauver to fight attempts to weaken its bill, and if that bill should be reported out in what the drug industry considered an inoffensive form, the Senate Judiciary Committee would probably alter its version to more or less conform, on the ground that nothing stronger would be acceptable to the House.

Meanwhile, the Senate Judiciary Committee convened on Wednesday, June 6th, and the entire session was devoted to consideration of Kefauver's amendment on granting patents for combinations and modifications of existing drugs. Dirksen and Hruska proposed that instead of having to have "greater therapeutic effect," as S. 1552 stipulated, in order to be patented, a drug be required to have only a "substantial" advantage over its predecessors. This wording seemed imprecise to Kefauver, and he was insistent that the original wording be preserved, pointing out that Ladd, the Patent Commissioner, had approved it during the hearings. Dirksen and Hruska insisted that Ladd hadn't, so Kefauver said he would get a statement from him on the subject and present it at the next meeting, scheduled for the following Monday.

To Kefauver, the point was crucial. He suspected that if his opponents succeeded in watering down the patent amendment, their next move would be to dispense with it altogether. Then, since the bill would contain no patent prosions, they could argue that it was no longer a matter for the Judiciary Committee but should be passed on to the Labor and Public Welfare Committee, which would hold new hearings, and all this might well mean the end of the bill.

That afternoon, Kefauver went to see Ladd, who readily agreed to write a letter supporting his position. The letter was duly written, but, as it turned out, was to no purpose, for the White House had moved to resolve the conflict over the entire bill in its own way. One of the industry men involved explained it later on by saying, "The administration didn't want to antagonize Kefauver, the man on the white horse, but they wanted some kind of a bill and whatever credit for it they could get. Of course, they had to deal with Eastland, who, as chairman of Judiciary, would ultimately run the show. Some time earlier, the right-wingers in the industry had given Senator Eastland a terribly weak drug bill as a substitute for Kefauver's, but he had refused to go along with it, on the ground that if he took a bill like that to the floor, Kefauver would murder him. Well, when the White House decided to move, Feldman told Eastland that the President would like to see the drug bill reported out. Eastland was perfectly willing to coöperate, and the upshot was that one of Eastland's men, one of Dirksen's, one of Hruska's, and a couple of people from the Department of Health, Education, and Welfare would meet and settle things. Feldman asked whether he really meant to omit Kefauver, and Eastland replied that this omission was neces-

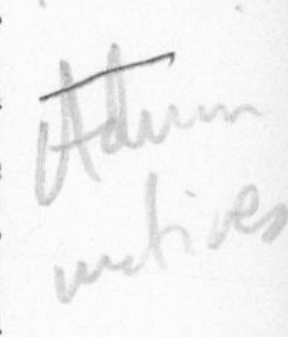

sary if the committee was to get some kind of bill out." In any case, later that day Feldman called Wilbur Cohen, H.E.W.'s assistant secretary for legislation. After outlining the situation, he asked Cohen to send a couple of technical advisers over to Eastland's office to work out a suitable compromise. Cohen assigned the task to Jerome Sonosky, who had drawn up the Harris bill, and to Theodore Ellenbogen, the F.D.A.'s legislative draftsman.

Although Sonosky had a fair idea of the purpose of Eastland's get-together, which later came to be known as "the secret meeting," he was not quite prepared for the participants in it. He and Ellenbogen arrived at the conference room of the Judiciary Committee at ten-thirty on the morning of June 8th to find no senators on hand. Those present, however, included not only Thomas Collins, Eastland's staff director, and Peter Chumbris and Ronald Raitt, minority counsels of the subcommittee, but also two men from the Pharmaceutical Manufacturers Association, Foley and Cutler, plus Cutler's partner Marshall Hornblower. (The presence of special-interest representatives in such a meeting is, if not unique, rare, for ordinarily everyone prefers a little more discretion when it comes to suggesting where the power lies. "It must be recognized that Congress does not lead in settling questions of public, political, or economic policy," the Legislative Committee of the American Legion reported at an annual convention some years ago. "Legislation is literally made outside the halls of Congress by groups of persons interested in legislation, mainly with economic motives, and the deliberative process within Congress constitutes a sort of formal ratification.")

As soon as Sonosky glanced over the amendments this

group proposed, he knew he was in for a bad day. "During the Kefauver hearings, the industry kept agreeing that some corrective measures were needed," he remarked afterward, "but when I saw their amendments, I realized just how far they meant to go toward remedying the abuses—not an inch!" His duty, as he saw it, was to bring the P.M.A. provisions into line with the President's Consumer Message—no small matter. "We battled back and forth and yelled and swore at each other, but still there was a good deal of give and take," he said. "By the time we finished, I had managed to get some good things added to the bill. At least, there were no steps backward."

About the best that could be said for the new bill, Kefauver remarked later, was that it didn't repeal the Food, Drug, and Cosmetic Act of 1938. In place of S. 1552's registration provision was one stating merely that all drug manufacturers were required to file their names and addresses with the F.D.A., and though another provision called for drug companies to be inspected at least once every two years, it set no inspection standards beyond stipulating that quality-control measures meet "current good manufacturing practice"—a phrase so vague as to cloud any attempt at juridical interpretation. The F.D.A. was not required to extend its certification to antibiotics to the newer antibiotics. There was an efficacy provision, but, unlike Kefauver's, it would not prevent a product that had been approved as effective for one purpose from being sold for any number of other purposes, with no need to furnish proof of its efficacy in the new fields. The problem of generic names was left entirely up to the Secretary of Health, Education, and Welfare, putting him in an awkward position, for with nothing set down in the bill to guide him, he would be subject to endless pressure from the industry. Finally, there was nothing at all on drug advertising.

VII A meeting of the Judiciary Committee was scheduled for the morning of Monday, June 11th, and as Kefauver, knowing nothing about the secret meeting and the secret bill, headed for the conference room, he felt quite confident about his chances of getting S. 1552 reported out that day—minus, of course, its compulsory-licensing and antitrust provisions. He expected the four Democrats on his subcommittee to stand by him; he thought it far from unlikely that at least two of his opponents would be absent, since that often happened; and he believed that in that event he could probably pick up the two votes necessary to swing the balance. He was particularly hopeful about getting his way in the matter of limiting patents for modifications and combinations of drugs. "I have McClellan's support, since he voted for it in his subcommittee," he said at the time. "I have Ladd's letter, and I understand that Eastland will go along with me. I've asked him two or three times if he meant to vote with me, and he said he did." When Kefauver entered the conference room, he was surprised to find all the members, except Senator Johnston. He was also surprised to see that Sonosky was present, but Eastland explained that he had asked H.E.W. to send over a technical adviser.

As soon as the meeting was called to order, Kefauver presented Ladd's letter and asked for a vote on the question of retaining his original wording on the amendment on patenting modifications and combinations. To his amazement, both

Eastland and McClellan joined the opposition, making it nine strong and leaving only Hart, Dodd, Carroll, and Long on his side. The moment the original wording was voted down, Dirksen moved to replace the amendment with one stipulating that H.E.W. be permitted to supply information on modified or combined drugs if the Patent Office asked for it. On this, the vote was ten to three in favor, for Dodd had left to attend to other matters, and Long had defected. This left the bill with that one slim patent amendment, which was the only thing that preserved the committee's jurisdiction over it. If this jurisdiction was now a bit shaky, however, Kefauver's opponents had no intention of trying to refer the whole question of drugs to another committee; they were doing splendidly in the Judiciary Committee.

When the second vote had been tallied, Dirksen casually put mimeographed copies of the new S. 1552—the Eastland-Dirksen bill, as it came to be known—on the table and explained that it contained some revisions of Kefauver's F.D.A. amendments. Kefauver was stunned. He demanded time to study the new bill. Eastland granted him as much, and Kefauver went into a huddle with Hart and Carroll. Now and then, as they read through the bill, Carroll asked Sonosky whether he spoke for the administration. Each time, Sonosky replied that he represented H.E.W., and that he had attended the meeting solely as a technical adviser. This answer satisfied no one, and finally Kefauver insisted on a yes or no, whereupon Sonosky told him that his superiors in H.E.W. had directed him to attend the secret meeting but that they had not seen the resulting bill.

Kefauver went out into an adjoining office, telephoned Feldman, and asked what part he had had in the secret meeting. "He said that he knew nothing about it, and that the White House backed me to the letter," Kefauver said later. "Then I phoned Cohen, and he said that he'd been asked to send someone to the meeting but that he knew nothing about the amendments. I told him, 'It looks to me as though you were working both sides of the street. This is the first time in my twenty-three years in Congress that an administration has emasculated a bill without letting its sponsor and chairman know.' "

Back in the conference room, Kefauver asked Sonosky if he spoke for Cohen. Sonosky answered that he had shown the amendments to Cohen but not in their final form. "How can that be true?" Kefauver demanded. "I just talked to Cohen, and he said he knew nothing about the amendments." Sonosky shrugged, and said nothing.

Soon afterward, Eastland indicated that he was ready to move for a vote on the bill, and at that Carroll, who had been on the Judiciary Committee long enough to learn something about filibustering whenever a civil-rights measure came up, took the floor and held forth until noon, when the Senate was officially in session. Then, as the Senate rules permit, he objected to the continuation of the meeting.

"I've never been so disturbed by double dealing in all my life," Kefauver said afterward. "I trusted those people. They've obviously decided that it would be better to get *some* kind of a bill—the weakest possible—passed now. That way, it will be another twenty-five years before anything more is done. And if they get this new bill through, they can say to the public, 'The industry was investigated thoroughly and Congress did such and such. Now you can have complete faith in drugs again.' Also, I think it was the feeling on the part of the administration, especially the F.D.A., that they didn't want many reforms to start with. This new bill shows that they were content with the most moderate improvements. Now they can claim that they got legislation through to protect the people. At the same time, they can say to the industry, 'See, we didn't do you much harm.' "

VIII

Back in his office, Kefauver sat down heavily in the red leather armchair behind his desk and stared at the wall. He had sent Blair and Horace Flurry, the subcommittee's senior counsel, off to study the new bill, but Fensterwald, his staff director, was with him, sitting in silence in a club chair opposite. For several minutes, Kefauver didn't speak. Then he said, "I'm going to the floor and have this out."

He started to get up, but Fensterwald said, "You'd better cool off first, boss. Anyway, we should have whatever you're going to say down on paper."

Kefauver thought for a few moments more, and then nodded. "O.K., let's put something together," he said, and phoned Caldwell, who was having lunch at the home of a friend nearby.

"How soon can you get back here, Charlie?" Kefauver asked.

"Practically immediately," Caldwell answered. "What happened?"

"They just chopped up the drug bill," Kefauver said.

Fensterwald went back to his office, a few doors down the hall, and started work on a speech. After a few minutes, he called Blair and asked if the bill was as bad as they had thought.

"It's worse," Blair replied.

Shortly afterward, Caldwell arrived, and he and Fensterwald completed a first draft. When they had finished it, they took it to Kefauver's office, and the Senator made a number of changes in it and added some new points. Then, at about two o'clock, as the three men left the Senator's office to take the subway to the Capitol, a buzzer rang twice, signifying a quorum call on the Senate floor. As staff members, Caldwell and Fensterwald had floor passes, and they took seats in the rear of the chamber. The chamber was beginning to fill up, and Kefauver told Senator Mike Mansfield, the Majority Leader, that he wanted to make a brief speech. Mansfield replied that a vote on the Interior Department's annual appropriation was just about to come up, and asked him to wait until it was over. "No," Kefauver said. "I want to do it now." More than fifty senators were present, and he wanted them to hear what he had to say.

When a senator is scheduled to make a speech, his name is put on a list, and the White House is immediately notified by ticker. A few minutes after Kefauver had spoken to Mansfield, a page informed Kefauver that he had a telephone call from the White House. The caller was Feldman, and he wanted to know what the Senator intended to say. When Kefauver gave him a general outline, Feldman said that the speech would put him in an embarrassing position in relation to the President. Kefauver politely heard him out, then retorted, "I haven't been so shoddily treated in twenty-three years in Congress," and hung up. Upon his return to the chamber, Robert G. Baker, secretary to the majority, hurried over to him and urged him to postpone his speech. Again Kefauver refused.

Ordinarily whenever enough senators are on hand in the chamber to create a hubbub, there is one. There was one on this occasion, too, but as soon as Kefauver was recognized by the chair and began, "Mr. President, today a severe blow to the public interest was delivered in the Senate Judiciary Committee," his colleagues began to quiet down. "Most of the drug-manufacturing industry and its acolytes have been punching away for some time at S. 1552, which is designed to make vital prescription drugs available to the people at reasonable prices," he continued. "Today, they swung a haymaker and just about knocked this bill right out of the ring." At the word "acolyte," Hruska picked up a pencil and jotted a note on a pad before him at his desk on the extreme right of the Republican side. Eastland, lounging in his seat, looked amused as Kefauver went on, "I think the time has come for the spotlight to be turned on so that the people of this country can see who is on which side." After an account of his two-and-a-half-year struggle to get effective regulation of the drug industry, Kefauver inserted into the record both President Kennedy's letter to Eastland and Ladd's letter to Kefauver. "Having received this endorsement of the Commissioner of Patents, I felt that this provision would cause no more controversy," Kefauver said. "Much to my amazement, at a meeting of the Judiciary Committee this morning, I discovered that there had been a secret meeting between representatives of the Department of Health, Education, and Welfare —just how much authority the representatives there had I do not know—and staff members of the Antitrust Subcommittee representing the Senator from Mississippi [Eastland] and staff members of the Antitrust Subcommittee representing the Senator from Illinois [Dirksen] and the Senator from Nebraska [Hruska], of which I knew nothing. . . . Not only had there been an agreement to eliminate the remaining patent provision endorsed by Commissioner Ladd, but there had also been an agreement to water down virtually every remaining feature of the bill. . . . I was surprised and put out that I, as chief sponsor of the bill, had neither been invited to the meeting nor knew anything about it. The bill which now remains is a mere shadow of the one approved by the Antitrust and Monopoly Subcommittee only a few months ago. I have had many inquiries as to what is happening about drugs—when prices are going down, when we are going to have more accurate advertising, when we are going to have safer drugs. I want the people to know what has been happening and what the situation is. The bill as it stands is admittedly agreeable to the Senator from Illinois and the Senator from Nebraska. They have generally, and I think admittedly, taken the position on these issues set forth by the pharmaceutical manufacturing industry."

Although some members of Kefauver's staff had wanted him to attack not only Dirksen and Hruska directly but the President, too, as an old pro and a strong party man, he preferred to approach that problem obliquely. (Moreover, he was well aware of the political maxim stated in *Profiles in Courage*—that "in these days of Civil Service, the loaves and fishes available to the legislator are comparatively few; and he who breaks the party's rules may find that there are suddenly none at all.") On three different occasions, he said, in one way or another, that he couldn't believe "there has been any backing away on the part of the President of the United States," and then demanded confirmation of that belief by concluding, "In view of the fact that representatives of the Department of Health, Education, and Welfare participated in secret meetings to damage this bill seriously, I think the people are now entitled to know just how they happened to be there and what the administration's present position is."

When Kefauver sat down, the chamber was silent for a good half a minute. Senator Albert Gore, his junior colleague from Tennessee, had moved nearer to hear what Kefauver was saying, and at the end he stood there for a few moments, staring in wonder at his senior. A few days later, Murray Kempton read Kefauver's speech in the Congressional Record, and reacted much the same way. "The passion of his grievance was unprecedented, both in a man so mild and in a loyal Democrat," he wrote in the New York *Post*. Far more, it was practically unprecedented for anyone to attack both the leader of his party and the chairman of a committee he belongs to, especially someone like Eastland, who is a man of considerable power in the Senate. As chairman of the Judiciary Committee, through which roughly half of all the Senate's business passes, he has such influence and prestige that he has more than once been called the king of kings among committee chairmen.

It was reported later that the Senate "club"—the informal alliance between the dozen or so "establishmentarians" of both parties who more or less run the Senate—was outraged by Kefauver's violation of its basic rule: take any defeat gracefully and, above all, in silence. However, his attack was received by some of his colleagues with a good deal of pleasure. Senator Paul Douglas said, "I don't remember anything quite like it happening in the Senate before. And, if you ask me, it was about time."

As soon as Kefauver sat down, Eastland rose. "I accept full responsibility for the alleged secret meeting which the Senator from Tennessee describes," he said. "The truth is that the administration designated certain individuals to handle the drug bill. The Senator from Tennessee would offer amendments, and would get two or three votes, out of a committee of fifteen members. It was my obligation to do what I think was needed to get a realistic drug program, so I asked those who represented the administration to meet with the staff of the Judiciary Committee and to meet with the staffs of senators who opposed the bill or who opposed parts of the bill, to see if, within the President's letter to me, we could arrive at a drug bill both healthy and wholesome, which would be a step forward. That was done. It was agreed on. I admit that I did not call in my friend from Tennessee for consultation, because I thought it would be a futile act. I did not think he would make any agreement with respect to anything."

Having had his say, Eastland took a cigar out of his pocket and sauntered out to the Democratic cloakroom. As he did, Hruska got the floor, and, stabbing the air with a forefinger, shouted, "I am as concerned as anyone about proper use of drugs by those who are ill, those who need relief from pain, and those whose lives could be saved through them. I am deeply in sympathy with the declared objectives of the bill. . . . Any inference [*sic*] that the senator from Nebraska or the senator from Illinois represents the American Pharmaceutical Association [*sic*], if that was what the senator from Tennessee was making, would be seriously mistaken and deeply resented. My concern is for the consumer of the drug."

Senator Maurine Neuberger, a Democrat from Oregon and one of Kefauver's allies on most issues, listened to Hruska, and then bent over her desk, laughing silently. A few desks away, Senator Douglas watched the proceedings with obvious relish. At several points during the ensuing debate, he broke into a smile, and once, when Hruska and Eastland conferred briefly in the aisle separating the two parties, he laughed outright. "It was the most explicit illustration of the coalition at work I'd ever seen," he remarked later. "All pretense had suddenly vanished."

Carroll was almost as angry as Kefauver about the secret meeting, but during the first part of the debate, he showed no inclination to participate. Suddenly, though, he jumped to his feet and, not waiting for recognition from the chair, went to Kefauver's aid. "I believe the Senator from Tennessee is fully justified in asking the President where he stands and asking H.E.W. where they stand," he said angrily, "and to find out if a couple of ribbon clerks [from H.E.W.] who have no real technical knowledge of the bill can draw up a bill without having had any kind of knowledge of this kind of work!"

Hruska tried to interrupt him, but Carroll refused to yield the floor he didn't have, though he did calm down a bit. "I wish to say a word for the senior Senator from Mississippi, the Chairman of the Committee on the Judiciary," he went on. "I believe he was acting in good faith. I think he wants to get a bill. I felt then, and it is my feeling now, that he thought in order to get a bill he would have to do it in this fashion. I think that was an error of judgment. I see nothing calculated or premeditated about it. He was not malicious. He wanted to get a bill out of committee. I believe the White House had been pressing him to report a bill on medical legislation. . . . We must not blame it all on the Republicans. Most of the Democrats voted that way, too. I did not question their motivation at all. We have enough experience to know that from time to time little coalitions are at work. . . . We are experienced enough to know the pitfalls of this type of legislation. We are hitting into one of the biggest industries of the nation—one with the highest prices, and one that is subject to the least regulation."

Apparently, someone had gone out to the cloakroom to let Eastland know what Carroll had said about him, for Eastland hurried back into the chamber and demanded, "Did the Senator from Colorado say that my judgment was bad in the matter?"

"I said the judgment of the Chairman of the Judiciary Committee was bad in not conferring with the Senator from Tennessee, and in not conferring with the other Democratic members of the committee," Carroll answered calmly.

"I think I used good judgment, because we have a bill which, as I understand, the administration favors," Eastland said. "What is wrong with an accomplishment? I had no interest in the bill."

"If this is the President's method of operating . . . I think we are entitled to know it!" Carroll shouted.

"It is not the President's method of operating," Eastland replied. "I have assumed full responsibility for the way the situation was handled, because the responsibility was placed upon me to get a bill."

Kefauver rose and said, "This morning, I called Mr. Cohen, the Undersecretary of Health, Education, and Welfare; but no official of the Department of Health, Education, and Welfare seemed to know anything about someone's being up here and working out amendments to the bill."

With a bland smile, Eastland retorted, "This afternoon, a high official of the Department of Health, Education, and Welfare told me—and I think that before this is over they will speak for themselves—that they favor it."

Kefauver wanted to know who had said this, but Eastland

refused to divulge the person's name, and went on to accuse Kefauver of mere "grandstand stuff for votes."

As Kefauver was about to protest, Carroll broke in again. "If the White House is telling the Chairman of the Senate Judiciary Committee one thing and is telling the Senator from Tennessee another," he shouted, waving his arms, "it is a helluva way to run a railroad!"

Then Senator Hart, a wryly articulate man who had been in the Senate for only three years, took the floor and said, "Mr. President, as the holder of parking license plate number eighty-five, my remarks will not reflect any sensitivity about failure to have consultation. I think I have not yet reached the stage where this situation affects my judgment." He went on to suggest that the bill offered that morning be inserted in the record, so that his colleagues would understand "the apprehension of some of us about the forthrightness with which it was proposed that we act." Remarking that whenever a liberal economic measure came up, some of his colleagues went off "like an automatic sprinkler system," Hart then drew an appreciative laugh from the civil-rights supporters, whose efforts Eastland always blocked, by concluding, "It has been suggested that in the Judiciary Committee one of the reasons why we cannot get out of committee bills in a certain area is that we have a very able Chairman. The converse is being demonstrated—that if the Chairman rules it, we can get other bills out. This also is a moral." (Hart was putting himself in some jeopardy—not just with Eastland but back home as well. Two of the country's largest drug firms, Upjohn and Parke, Davis, were located in Michigan, and word was going around the state that his support of S. 1552 was endangering the jobs of thousands of his constituents, and that if he and Kefauver were successful, some local drug plants might have to be shut down.)

When, after nearly two hours, the debate was on the verge of expiring, Dirksen got up and said, "Mr. President, I hope my distinguished friend from Tennessee will do me the honor to give me a little attention. I have great affection for him. I like his relentlessness. He is as single-purposed as an Apache Indian. He is as gracious as a Victorian lady. There is a rare diligence about him, and a rare consistency also. The difficulty is that we do not agree on the fundamental thesis. I am glad he is a patient man when he essays to change the result. His patience is certainly equal to that of Job. I think he makes Job look a little like an amateur."

IX

For a time, it appeared that Kefauver's denunciation of the secret meeting would do him more harm than good, for he had not been willing to wait for his staff to prepare a press release, and when he delivered his speech, there were few reporters in the press gallery. Accordingly, the debate—which was generally considered to be one of the bitterest to take place in the Senate in some years—did not immediately become known to the public, although the New York *Post* picked it up, in a story by Barbara Yuncker, which quoted a high official of H.E.W. as saying that the administration could "live with" the new bill. Within a few days, however, word of the secret meeting began to spread, and eventually a number of other papers mentioned it, including the New York *Times*. In an editorial on the secret meeting, which it called "a bizarre method of revision," the *Times* said, "The President has plenty of problems to occupy him these days, but this is a matter of sufficient moment to justify a clear statement from the White House as to which version meets the President's tests as outlined in his April letter [to Eastland]."

As Miss Yuncker's source later admitted privately, it appeared that Kefauver's speech had got just enough notice to stop his opponents short. "If he hadn't made it, the revised drug bill would probably have sailed through Congress," the man said. "But now it looks as if there won't be any drug law this year—at least, not one that's backed by the administration. After all, why should we take the new bill to the Senate floor and give Kefauver an opportunity to get up and accuse us of allowing high-priced, dirty drugs to be sold?" Asked why the administration hadn't seen fit to answer Kefauver's charges through one of its Senate spokesmen if it felt that its actions were justified, he laughed and said, "Who *us?* Attack Estes Kefauver, the protector of the people?"

On June 19th, when the House Interstate and Foreign Commerce Committee began holding its hearings on the Harris bill, the opening witness, H.E.W. Secretary Abraham Ribicoff, confessed that the administration couldn't live with the Eastland-Dirksen bill after all. "I do not think that these amendments conform with the President's recommendations," he said when he was questioned about them.

"Do they substantially differ from what you have recommended here today?" Harris asked.

"I think they differ substantially enough to make us quite unhappy about them," Ribicoff answered.

Dirksen was furious at the administration for reneging on its earlier acceptance of the secret-meeting bill. Now he stood accused of taking the drug industry's side in its attempt to weaken S. 1552, and Representative Sidney Yates, his opponent in the forthcoming election, was out in Illinois making political capital out of the charge. When a reporter mentioned to Dirksen that he had been accused in the past of taking the part of business interests in general, and asked if the charge, in this case, were not equally true of the administration, Dirksen nodded emphatically. "It certainly is!" he said.

In his column, Murray Kempton had written, "The Administration may, in the end, find itself with no bill at all. Kefauver remains a powerful figure, and he is a patient, although never malicious, enemy. If the bill which Health, Education, and Welfare has accepted seems to him maimed beyond recovery, he is strong enough to put it out of its misery if he chooses." As it turned out, Kefauver did not so choose. He voted for it in committee, with the warning that he meant to do his best to strengthen it when it came up for a vote in the Senate. "It's strange how differently some people act in the dark privacy of a committee meeting and the public glare of the Senate floor," he explained.

On July 12th, Eastland convened the committee to take what he assumed was a final vote on the revised S. 1552. All fifteen members were on hand, and when the tally was in, the only vote against the bill was Eastland's. Kefauver quickly grasped Eastland's purpose in voting against the bill, which was to avoid serving as its floor manager, with the probable result that Kefauver himself, as sponsor of the original measure, would have to; if he was its manager, he saw, he would be effectually restrained from attacking the bill. Accordingly, he pointed out to the committee that only fifty-five lines of his bill remained in S. 1552 as it stood, and that therefore he would have to refuse any offer to manage it on the floor. Eastland then called for another vote, and this time it was unanimous. On July 19th, the bill was officially reported out.

The general feeling in Washington now was that S. 1552 was dead for that session. In the face of Kefauver's vocal opposition, the administration was not disposed to press for passage of the weakened bill, nor, it seemed, could the White House gracefully get behind Kefauver's original measure now, even if it wanted to. The only hope Kefauver had was that Celler would be able to pry his version of S. 1552 out of his committee, and that possibility seemed extremely remote, because a majority of the committee's members were unwilling to antagonize Harris, who traditionally had jurisdiction over all F.D.A. matters.

"It would be very difficult to get that bill out of my committee right now," Celler admitted. "I'm waiting to see what happens on the Senate side. Kefauver's bill has been very watered down over there, and I'm not interested in pushing through bad legislation. If S. 1552 is strengthened on the floor, then I'll try to get my bill out of committee. But the chances of strong action in the Senate don't look good. Without the support of the administration, it's hopeless, and the administration hasn't been supporting the Kefauver bill."

X In mid-July, Dr. Robert P. Fischelis, the columnist for the *American Druggist* wrote, "It took a catastrophe to put the teeth into the present Food, Drug, and Cosmetic Act and it begins to look as though something like this may have to happen again before consumer pressure will be exerted in sufficient intensity to move Congress to take necessary action."

The catastrophe he was referring to occurred in 1937—four years after Senator Royal S. Copeland, a physician and former Commissioner of Health in New York City, had introduced a strong drug bill, which had been lying around Congress ever since. It was in mid-1937 that sulfanilamide hit the market, and within a few months of that event a salesman for one of the companies that produced it happened to tell a chemist at the company's plant that he could sell a great deal more of the drug if it could be made available in a liquid form, for patients who were unable to take capsules. The chemist went to work on the problem, and before long he came up with a solvent that did the trick—diethylene glycol, a glycerine-like by-product of petroleum refining. In September, he mixed up fifty-eight and a half pounds of sulfanilamide, sixty gallons of diethylene glycol, and eighty gallons of water, and added some sweetening, which he tested by taking a sip or two, and some coloring. He put the mixture up in small brown bottles, labeled them "Elixir Sulfanilamide," and shipped them out to his distributors. On October 11th, while the company was preparing more of the concoction, the deaths of six people in Tulsa were traced to the diethylene glycol that had been used as a solvent for sulfanilamide. Soon, several more people died after using the "elixir," and the company began trying to collect all the bottles of it that were on the market. At that point, the government moved in, assigning all its food-and-drug inspectors to round up the deadly stuff. Under the existing law, the Food and Drug Administration had no control over even the safety of drugs, but, as it happened, the use of the word "elixir" technically implied that the solvent involved was alcohol, rather than diethylene glycol, and the government did have something to say about misbranding. When it was all over, a hundred and eight people were dead—a hundred and seven patients, who had taken the "elixir," and the chemist, who had killed himself.

At the time of the tragedy, Dr. Fischelis was editor of the New Jersey *Journal of Pharmacy* and in a lead editorial entitled "Have They Died in Vain?" he wrote:

> The medical profession has been entirely too ready to rely upon advertising claims for drug products without requiring scientific proof of therapeutic value and safety. The drug manufacturing industry has been entirely too eager to produce products for profit without due regard for the hazards involved in combining drugs without complete knowledge of the effect of such combinations. . . . Lawmakers have been entirely too ready to listen to and act upon the arguments of constituents with a personal interest in the emasculation of laws and regulations which would provide the kind of control that is in the best interests of the public. . . . Let the industry now show whether it is dominated by dollars or by some conception of the responsibility that goes with the production of agents directly affecting human lives. It is not sufficient to say "We believe in strong food and drug laws" and then offer all kinds of amendments and changes in wording specifically designed to weaken governmental control over the very things that close the door to fraud and quackery.

Shortly afterward, the Department of Agriculture, of which the F.D.A. was then a part, issued a report on the calamity to Congress, concluding, "A few simple and inexpensive tests on experimental animals would have quickly demonstrated the toxic properties of both diethylene glycol and the 'elixir.'" The public was outraged, and so, finally, were its representatives; in June of 1938 they passed a good part of what Copeland had asked for.

The day that S. 1552 was approved by the Judiciary Committee, Bernard Nossiter, the chief economics writer for the

Washington *Post*, stopped off at Blair's office to commiserate with him on the demise of the drug bill. "Don't be too sure," Blair told him. By this time, Mrs. Wendt had completed her dossier on thalidomide, and Blair told Nossiter about some of the things she had found out. Her most striking discovery was that the drug would almost certainly have been approved if it had not been for a woman physician, Frances O. Kelsey, who was a medical officer on the staff of the F.D.A. Dr. Kelsey, it appeared, had steadfastly refused to approve thalidomide on the ground that it hadn't been properly tested. "If it hadn't been for Dr. Kelsey," Blair said, "thalidomide would have been selling here for the past year, and we'd now have a medical disaster of major proportions on our hands."

When Nossiter got back to his office, he mentioned the incident to Seymour Fishbein, an assistant city editor, and the next day Fishbein asked Morton Mintz, one of the *Post*'s top reporters, to look into it. Mintz went to see Dr. Kelsey, who answered his questions in a forthright and undramatic manner. She and her husband had been professors at the University of South Dakota School of Medicine, she said, and had moved to Washington in 1960—she to take up her present job, and he to become a special assistant to the Surgeon General. On September 12, 1960, she had got her first big assignment—Merrell's application to market thalidomide, under the trade name Kevadon. The data accompanying the application—based largely on experience with the drug in West Germany, where it had been widely used without apparent ill effects for a couple of years—did not impress her, because she had often seen a drug acclaimed for a comparable period, only to learn later that it had harmful side effects. Her doubts about thalidomide increased when she discovered from Merrell's data that although the drug made human beings exceedingly sleepy, it had no observable effect of any sort on animals, even in huge doses. Under the existing law—and this, of course, was one of Kefauver's big objections to it—the F.D.A. was required to hand down its decision on a new drug within sixty days; otherwise its approval was automatic. There was one loophole, though—the F.D.A. medical officer could tell the manufacturer that his application was incomplete, and ask for more details. Each time the sixty-day deadline came up, Dr. Kelsey did just that in order to look into thalidomide further. Then, in February of 1961, she read, in a two-month-old issue of the *British Medical Journal,* a letter from a doctor suggesting that some recent cases of peripheral neuritis—a tingling sensation in the extremities—might have been caused by thalidomide. During the Second World War, Dr. Kelsey, in the course of doing extensive research on the effects of quinine on rabbits, had discovered that drugs that irritated adult nerves could cause paralysis, stunted growth, and deformity in the fetus, so the possible relationship between thalidomide and peripheral neuritis struck her as ominous. She immediately called this news to the attention of the Merrell people, and they reported that they had conducted tests that showed cases of peripheral neuritis resulting from the use of thalidomide to be extremely rare—roughly one in every three hundred thousand patients—and that also showed that the effect was reversible once the drug was discontinued. In April, Merrell's application to sell Kevadon in Canada was approved by the Canadian equivalent of the F.D.A., and the company stepped up its appeals to Dr. Kelsey.

About the same time, physicians in West Germany were

frantically searching for the source of an epidemic of phocomelia there, and reports were trickling in about malformed babies being born in Great Britain, Sweden, Italy, Switzerland, Lebanon, Israel, Australia, Brazil, and Peru. Doctors studied such possible causes as blood incompatibility between parents, radioactive fallout, detergents, X-rays, food preservatives, and a variety of other plausible factors, but got nowhere. Finally, Dr. Widikund Lenz, a Hamburg pediatrician, asked a number of mothers of deformed infants to fill out a questionnaire on what medication they had taken during pregnancy; a tabulation showed that some twenty per cent of them had taken Contergan, a trade name for thalidomide used by Chemie Grunenthal, the West German discoverers of the drug. Dr. Lenz then questioned all of the mothers again, specifically asking them about Contergan. This time, the figure rose to fifty per cent; the balance of the women who now mentioned it had neglected to list the drug the first time, they explained, because they had felt it was too commonplace—practically like aspirin—to be of any importance. In some of the remaining fifty per cent of the cases studied it was impossible to determine whether a woman with a deformed child had, in fact, taken thalidomide, for Grunenthal had sold it not only as a sleeping pill but in combination with aspirin, cough syrup, and other non-prescription medications.

On November 15th, Dr. Lenz warned Grunenthal about his suspicions. Five days later, at a meeting of pediatricians in Düsseldorf, he announced that he suspected a specific drug had caused the outbreak of phocomelia, but refrained from identifying it further than to say that it was a sleeping potion. At the end of his speech, another physician came up to him, and said, "Will you tell me confidentially is the drug Contergan? I ask because we have such a child and my wife took Contergan." Dr. Lenz told him that it was.

About the same time, Dr. W. G. McBride, a pediatrician in New South Wales, Australia, saw three infants with phocomelia in April and three more in October and November. He found that all six mothers had taken Distaval, the British brand of thalidomide. On November 27th, the Australian branch of Distillers Ltd., the English firm under license from Grunenthal to produce thalidomide, cabled its home office in London about Dr. McBride's findings. News of this reached a physician in Stirlingshire, Scotland, who began reviewing ten cases of phocomelia that he had seen; eight of the mothers, he found, recalled taking Distaval. A German obstetrician, hearing about Dr. Lenz's suspicions, was unconvinced, so he asked sixty-five of his patients who were pregnant if they had taken Contergan; only one had, and when only she gave birth to a deformed child, he was convinced.

Later that November, Grunenthal withdrew all forms of thalidomide from distribution and sale, and informed its foreign licensees of its action. Although Distillers Ltd. withdrew the drug from the British market on December 2, 1961, Merrell did not withdraw it from the Canadian market until three months later, on March 2, 1962. Six days after that, on March 8th, the firm withdrew its F.D.A. application.

Mintz's story appeared on the front page of the Washington *Post* for Sunday, July 15th, under the headline "HEROINE OF FDA KEEPS BAD DRUG OFF MARKET." On July 16th, Kefauver released Mrs. Wendt's dossier on thalidomide to the press, and on July 18th, speaking in the Senate, he recommended that Dr. Kelsey be awarded the gold medal for Distinguished Federal Civilian Service, and went on to remind his listeners of measures to protect the American people against just such disasters that had been included in S. 1552 before Eastland and Dirksen honed it down. (Although Kefauver was ultimately successful in linking his bill and the thalidomide scare in the public mind, S. 1552 actually did nothing to facilitate the F.D.A.'s efforts to obtain information about new drugs. On the other hand, it did give the F.D.A. open-end authority; that is, it abolished the time limit after which approval became automatic.)

The press buildup was accelerated on July 25th, when a Phoenix housewife, Mrs. Robert Finkbine, who was then pregnant and who discovered that she had been taking thalidomide in the form of Distaval, bought in England by her husband, announced that she would try to get a legal abortion. Ultimately she did—not here, but in Sweden—and the doctor who performed the operation announced that the fetus was, indeed, deformed. "Will the administration give Senator Kefauver some support on this issue and not confine itself to generalities about its concern for consumers?" The New York *Times* asked the following day.

On July 27th, a news story distributed by United Press International revealed that, according to Commissioner Larrick of the F.D.A., Merrell had sent thalidomide to more than twelve hundred doctors for testing, and it later turned out that not all the supplies had been recovered. In a follow-up story, the Associated Press pointed out that such testing could be carried on with almost no government supervision; a drug company was required only to keep records of its shipments of experimental drugs, and to label them "Caution, New Drug Limited by Federal Law to Investigative Use." As for a physician who received one of these shipments, he was required to do nothing beyond sending the company a statement, signed by him, to the effect that he was qualified to test the drug; no standards existed for determining whether his opinion was justified. Nor, it turned out, was the physician required to inform patients to whom he gave the drug that it was experimental.

No amount of detective work at the time—or today, for that matter—could show how many deformed infants were born as a result of the experimental use of thalidomide in this country, for neither hospitals nor individual doctors have ever been required to report the birth of malformed children. Besides, many physicians, it was eventually learned, had kept incomplete records of the women to whom they had given thalidomide, and those whose records were impeccable could scarcely be expected to notify the press that they had been instrumental in causing phocomelia.

On July 24th, Kefauver made public a letter he had sent to President Kennedy urging him to award Dr. Kelsey a gold medal for her services. Then, three days later, he went off on a tangent that was to end up in a heated wrangle with the administration over its so-called satellite bill—a measure to allow a private corporation, in which individuals would own only half the stock, the other half being held by private communications companies, to operate a global communications system based on relaying devices such as Telstar. Everyone assumed, of course, that the corporation would ultimately be controlled by A.T.&T., which was already the largest private monopoly in the world. Although Telstar had been developed by Bell Laboratories, a subsidiary of A.T.&T., the rockets that boosted it aloft had cost the taxpayers upwards of twenty billion dollars, and a number of liberals in the Senate felt that the government had not only the right but the duty to protect the public's investment. Some of them proposed outright government ownership, as in the T.V.A., while others, including Kefauver, proposed that the government keep close control over the use of all satellites, as it had with atomic energy. By late July, when the administration was ready to call for a vote on the bill, there had been little debate over it in Congress or anywhere else—particularly in the press, which led Senator Wayne Morse, of Oregon, to charge that there had been a press blackout on the subject. In any event, Morse, Kefauver, and a handful of other senators resolved to filibuster against the bill, in an effort to bring their case to the public. For five days, beginning July 27th, they did filibuster, and at the close of the fifth day, by unanimous consent of the Senate, the bill was sent to the Senate Committee on Foreign Relations, which promised to look into one of the filibusterers' objections—that, in effect, the satellite corporation would be in the position of negotiating treaties with foreign governments.

President Kennedy was strongly opposed to the filibusterers. On the other hand, former President Truman strongly supported them. "I don't think the President understands the bill," Truman told reporters. "The damned Republicans and some Democrats are trying to give away public property."

On the morning of August 1st, the day that the satellite bill was sent to the Foreign Relations Committee, Senator Hubert H. Humphrey, Majority Whip, held a three-hour hearing of his Subcommittee on Reorganization and International Organization to study "inter-agency coördination in drug research information." Despite the unresounding purpose, the hearing room was overflowing with spectators, reporters, and television crewmen, for the star witness was Dr. Kelsey. Humphrey stuck to the subject announced, but his Republican colleagues—Senators Karl E. Mundt, of South Dakota, and Jacob K. Javits, of New York—were more interested in the general problem that thalidomide had raised. Commissioner Larrick was the leadoff witness, and once Mundt had led him to concede that the government had no control over which or how many doctors tested drugs, or, in fact, over how many people they were tested on, he said, "Well, now, in simple talk it seems to me this is a loophole in the law through which you could drive a South Dakota wagonload of hay. . . . It would seem to me just ordinary prudence would say at this stage, 'Now, yes, you can have *some* experts, but you can have only ten, and they can have just a limited amount of drugs, and we want to see what the reaction is on human beings, on the world's most expensive variety of guinea pigs, before you can spread it out over an unlimited number."

On the dais in front of Humphrey was a file containing some F.D.A. material relating to thalidomide, among it a ten-page, single-spaced document describing the day-by-day communications between Merrell and the F.D.A. on the subject of Kevadon. Altogether the document listed fifty instances where the company had contacted either Dr. Kelsey or her superiors in its attempt to get the drug approved. On one occasion, the chronology stated, Merrell's representative had objected to a letter from Dr. Kelsey as being "somewhat libelous" (which had unsettled her so that she later consulted a lawyer to find out what her liability was, if any), and on another occasion—the day that Dr. Lenz informed Grunenthal about his suspicions, as it happened—Merrell had pressed her for a decision because they hoped "to get the product on the market by Christmas."

For some reason, Humphrey didn't mention the F.D.A. document, but Javits, who had learned of its contents from a man close to the F.D.A., was extremely interested in discussing the subject, although he had to approach things indirectly to avoid giving Humphrey the impression that he had actually read the paper. Turning to the subject of Merrell's contacts with Dr. Kelsey, who was seated at the witness table beside Larrick, he asked, "Did they come in very frequently and try to get this cleared?"

Dr. Kelsey hesitated. "Well, they did come in quite often," she said finally.

Javits was apparently dissatisfied with her response, for a few minutes later he returned to the subject. "And did you have any feeling that any effort was made to push you, rush you, pressure you into allowing [thalidomide] to be used commercially, notwithstanding these indicia [of side effects] which you had?"

Pausing again, Dr. Kelsey glanced at Larrick, who stared straight ahead. "Well," she answered at last, "I think they were very anxious, yes. And one can understand that it had wide use elsewhere."

Javits had also learned that although Grunenthal had withdrawn thalidomide from sale on November 28, 1961, Merrell had sent the doctors whom it had asked to test the drug warning letters a week later stating that information had come from abroad reporting "congenital malformations in the offspring of a few mothers who had taken thalidomide," and advising them not to give the drug to pregnant or premenopausal women. Not until three months later, he pointed out, had Merrell contacted the doctors involved and asked them either to return or destroy the supplies of thalidomide they still had.

When Javits asked Dr. Kelsey if she felt that there had been an undue time lag, she deferred to Larrick. "I think the firm proceeded with reasonable diligence to get the drug off the market," he said.

Javits turned back to Dr. Kelsey. "Well, now, Dr. Kelsey, did you feel that all of these actions were taken with due diligence—that is, as diligently as one could under the circumstances?" he asked.

Dr. Kelsey paused once more. Finally, her voice barely audible, she said, "Well, my understanding was when the drug was still in the investigational stage that the onus was on the company and that our authority did not extend there."

Javits gave up trying.

XI

Later that day, those who were pressing for the Kefauver drug bill got still another jolt. At a press conference that afternoon, President Kennedy made a statement to the effect that the version of S. 1552 that had been reported out by the Judiciary Committee did not go far enough toward fulfilling the recommendations contained in the Consumer Message. "I hope the members of Congress will adopt those more careful provisions contained in the administration bill, introduced by Congressman Oren Harris, of Arkansas, in the House," the President said. "The administration bill, for example, unlike the Senate Judiciary bill, will allow for immediate removal from the market of a new drug where there is an immediate hazard to public health, which cannot be done now, and contains with it many other very essential safeguards which I hope the Congress will act on this year."

Kefauver had gone to Tennessee to vote in the Democratic primary, and when members of his staff heard about the press conference, they quickly got together to discuss the kind of statement the Senator should make when he returned. As they saw it, the President's remarks amounted to a rejection of Kefauver's efforts. For one thing, the so-called Senate Judiciary bill had been approved by the administration, and, for another, taking a new drug off the market was by no means the same as preventing a drug that wasn't on the market from getting there. On the other hand, the Harris bill failed to abolish the automatic-approval provision of the law, and this, Blair felt, was of pivotal importance in giving medical officers sufficient time to evaluate new drug applications. (One of the men who had helped draft the President's statement was amused by Blair's subsequent attempts to correct the record on this point. "We were absolutely wrong factually," he said, "but we were absolutely right politically.")

When Kefauver got back to Washington that night, he joined several of his staff members in his office to wait for the primary returns to be phoned in from Tennessee. Upon being told about the press conference, he shook his head, lit a cigarette, and said, "Isn't that a hell of a thing—after all these years of work to get a slap in the face like that?" His aides suggested three different strategies: to attack the administration directly; to try to strengthen the Eastland-Dirksen bill on the floor; or to avoid antagonizing the President no matter what happened. Kefauver listened, asked a few questions, and then, toward midnight, got up and left without announcing any decision.

Unknown to the Kefauver camp, lights were also burning late over in the Department of Health, Education, and Welfare. On orders from the White House, Sonosky, Ellenbogen, and Winton B. Rankin, assistant commissioner of the F.D.A., were preparing still another drug bill for submission to the Senate. From one o'clock in the afternoon until three in the morning, they strengthened the Harris bill by adding parts of the Kefauver bill and some odds and ends of their own, and then they drew up a rough draft, consisting of seven amendments in all. Finally, they went home to get some sleep. They were up early the next morning, though, going over the draft, and at nine o'clock Sonosky hurried to the White House to see Theodore Sorensen, the President's special counsel, who examined the bill and gave it his approval. After that, Sorensen and Sonosky took a limousine over to the New Senate Office Building and went up to Eastland's office. Sorensen stayed around just long enough to make it clear that the President wanted the bill pushed through. Since the amendments brought the measure back fairly close to the one his committee had rejected, Eastland was left in the unhappy position of repudiating either his committee's handiwork or the President's. In view of the public's interest in the issue, he reluctantly decided that he must repudiate the committee's.

Later, Sonosky returned to his office, where he found Cohen waiting with word that the White House wanted them to draft explanations of the amendments, plus a covering letter to Eastland to be signed by the President. Both had to be ready by four-thirty that afternoon, Cohen said, because the President was due to leave for Hyannis Port at five. By a quarter after four, Sonosky and Cohen had a fairly complete draft of the explanations ready, along with the last paragraph of a two-paragraph letter, typed in position on a piece of White House stationery. They took a taxi to the White House, and during the short ride Cohen hastily wrote down a first paragraph on a scratch pad, finishing it just as they pulled up at the West Wing. They were ushered at once into the Oval Room, where President Kennedy greeted them and sat down to look over the two paragraphs of the letter. Without a word, he scribbled his signature below the typed paragraph, and then, looking up, said that it was imperative to finish up the rest at once. The public expected action, he added, and it had to be taken. Cohen explained that both the amendments and their explanations were still a bit rough and had to be rewritten. With a nod, the President said he would like all the work done by the following morning, so that it could be sent to him in Hyannis Port.

At about the same time, Kefauver decided on his strategy. A long talk with Mansfield and Humphrey had convinced him that the administration meant to support him, so he resolved not to challenge it either directly or indirectly. Humphrey had promised to help him push through some of his strengthening amendments, and Mansfield had said that the Democratic Policy Committee—the next obstacle in the legislative maze—would report out S. 1552 when it met the following Tuesday, August 7th, and that, with luck, the bill would get to the floor for a vote on Wednesday. Moreover, Kefauver had learned that Celler had convened his committee to see if he could get *his* version of the drug bill moving. Something that he didn't learn until later was that Harris, that same afternoon, had told an A.P. reporter that he had no intention of pushing for quick action on drug legislation. After remarking that the Senate had been considering the problem for three years, he concluded, "If they can't work anything out, I don't see why we should rack our brains."

That night, Sonosky, Ellenbogen, and three secretaries from the F.D.A. racked *their* brains in an effort to do all that the President had requested. They finished shortly after one o'clock, and Sonosky sent the results by messenger to the White House. At nine o'clock, after a few hours' sleep, he called the White House and dictated a press release to accompany the amendments. Apparently, someone decided that it might be unwise to keep Kefauver entirely in the dark again, so later that morning Mike N. Manatos, an administration legislative liaison man, telephoned him to say that some strong amendments to the Eastland-Dirksen bill were in the works. Kefauver, having no idea they were already completed, didn't ask to see them.

Since S. 1552 was already on the Senate calendar, Kefauver assumed that he and the other senators who had worked for strong drug legislation would be asked to offer the new amendments on the floor. As things turned out, however, the quest for public credit gave birth to a unique parliamentary tactic. On Sunday, August 5th, the President, in Hyannis Port, released the text both of the new amendments and of his letter to Eastland requesting that the Judiciary Committee recall the drug bill that it had reported out and incorporate the new amendments in it. In effect, this made it the President's bill. Kefauver's name was nowhere mentioned.

At ten-thirty on the following Tuesday morning, the Judiciary Committee met to have a look at the President's amendments, as the collage came to be called. On hand, besides the members and their aides, were Dr. Kelsey, Commissioner Larrick, Rankin, Sonosky, and Ellenbogen, all of them in the capacity of technical advisers. One of the amendments abolished automatic F.D.A. approval of new-drug applications, an idea that the committee had rejected out of hand only three weeks before; now it was quickly approved. Another amendment gave the Department of Health, Education, and Welfare the power to take a drug off the market without even a preliminary hearing if evidence showed it to be an imminent danger to the public health. Then, suddenly, several voices said at once that this took care of thalidomide, whereupon Eastland got up and indicated that the meeting was over.

Sonosky jumped to his feet. "No, gentlemen, this doesn't take care of thalidomide!" he said sternly. "And it doesn't take care of the President's other amendments, either." Everyone stared at him in astonishment, but he stood his ground, adding, "We have *not* finished, gentlemen."

Glaring at him, Hruska demanded, "Do you mean to say that we aren't interested in deformed babies?"

With a bewildered look, Sonosky shook his head. "I didn't say that," he answered.

"Yes, you did!" Hruska said. "You were looking directly at me."

"I'm sorry, Senator, but I wasn't," Sonosky retorted. Turning to Dirksen, he asked, "Was I, Senator?"

Dirksen shrugged, and Hruska cried, "All right, were you accusing me of not caring about deformed babies?"

Sonosky returned his angry look. "Well, Senator, if the shoe fits—" he said.

After a tense pause, Eastland said that the committee

would resume its study of the amendments the next day, and adjourned the meeting.

That afternoon, Kefauver went to the Senate floor with a brief speech that was intended to make it clear for the record where most of the President's amendments had come from. But before he could get the floor, Humphrey rose and said, "Once again, in the area of new drug legislation, the President has taken the initiative." The next morning, Humphrey and Mansfield attended a "leadership conference" at a White House breakfast, and that afternoon Mansfield emerged from the Policy Committee meeting and announced that the order of business would be the satellite bill, followed by the farm bill and the drug bill. On hearing the news, a Kefauver aide who was working on the satellite measure said, "If they think Estes is going to give up the satellite fight to get the drug bill through, they're crazy." A few minutes later, he sent the Senator a memorandum saying that he felt it was about time to blow the whistle on the administration, and suggesting that Kefauver take the floor and announce that he had no intention of making the trade implicitly offered but would fight against the first bill and for the other. Instead, Kefauver made his protest privately to Mansfield and Humphrey, saying to them, "This is a hell of a thing—putting monopoly welfare before the public welfare."

Over the next few days, the Judiciary Committee went on with its study of the new bill. It was slow, finicky work. Dirksen said later, "We argued about the touch of a word, the emphasis of a phrase, the striking out of a line, the replacing of a semicolon, and whether a comma was in the right place or whether a period ought to take its place." Kefauver began to despair of their ever getting anywhere, but then he was heartened by word from Celler that his committee was actually making some progress with its bill. Eventually, though, the conservatives there proved as balky as their Senate counterparts. (One of them, Representative George Meader, a Republican from Michigan, expressed a rather original view on the patent provision. "If patents are restricted as Kefauver wants, all drugs, including dangerous ones, will be cheaper and more widely available," he speculated. "That can only mean that more people will be harmed.") There was another complication, too. On the very day that Celler got his committee together, Harris unexpectedly announced that he would conduct further hearings on his bill beginning August 20th. Most people assumed that he had taken this step to warn off Celler, but actually he had been prompted to it, he admitted later, by a ten-minute telephone conversation with the President, who urged him to report out his bill.

The following day, the administration's position became cloudier than ever when Anthony J. Celebrezze, the new Secretary of H.E.W., issued a batch of regulations over drug testing. Among them were requirements that drug firms provide the F.D.A. with details about the distribution of new drugs for investigational use; that only qualified investigators be used, after their qualifications were filed with the government; that no new drugs be tested on human beings until they had been shown to be safe for animals; that the F.D.A. be kept fully informed of the progress of such testing; and that special precautions be taken with drugs intended for use by children or pregnant women. A good many people wondered why H.E.W. hadn't put out these regulations years ago if it had the power, and before long the P.M.A. pointed out that the new regulations "obviously reduce substantially the need for additional legislation."

Dirksen brought up the latter point on the floor of the Senate, and when he finished, Carroll flared up again. "I know who has been blocking the [drug] bill for many months," he shouted. "I know who has been playing the game of the pharmaceutical industry for months."

With a smile, Dirksen suggested that he name the person.

Ignoring the taunt, Carroll went on, "Those of whom I have spoken are intelligent senators. I have seen them cradle this corporation, that corporation, and this industry and that industry in my five years as a member of the Subcommittee on Antitrust and Monopoly. . . . The same procedure has been followed in respect to the drug bill. The record is clear to anyone who wishes to investigate."

On August 7th, the President awarded Dr. Kelsey a gold medal for distinguished government service, as Kefauver had suggested, but the White House press release made no mention of the Senator, declaring instead that the award had been made on the recommendation of the Secretary of H.E.W.—who, as it happened, wasn't in town at the time and knew nothing about the whole matter until afterward. "Washington is performing an act of contrition for bureaucratic fumbling and an almost total disinclination in the executive and legislative branches to press for higher ground than expediency in their decisions," wrote Doris Fleeson in her Washington *Evening Star* column on the White House award ceremony. At the last moment, the White House had invited Kefauver (described by Miss Fleeson as "one of the dread reformers who are decidedly out in today's Washington"), but when the press photographers went to work, he was elbowed aside in the crush.

XII By noon on Friday, August 10th, the Senate Judiciary Committee had accepted four of the new amendments more or less intact, so as soon as that day's meeting was over, Kefauver made his way to the Senate chamber, where the filibuster was due to be resumed. Obtaining the floor, he proceeded to test the leadership's position on the satellite bill versus the drug bill by pointing out that S. 1552 was already on the calendar and that only three of the President's amendments remained to be voted on, and asking for unanimous consent to consider the bill then and there. Mansfield quickly objected, and the filibuster continued.

Back in the Judiciary conference room, Eastland and Collins, his aide, were discussing how slowly the committee's consideration of the new drug bill was progressing. Now, Eastland remarked, it was going to stop altogether, for Morse had objected to any committee sessions while the Senate was convened, and to all appearances it looked as if it would be convened day and night until the matter was disposed of. After more discussion, however, Eastland came up with a novel parliamentary solution—namely, that the committee continue to meet without taking any votes; when everything was completed, he added, he would ask Mansfield to adjourn the Senate long enough for them to take one vote on the entire bill. Eastland asked Blair and Flurry, the subcommittee's senior counsel, to check it out with Kefauver and to let him know the outcome, adding that if Kefauver consented, they would meet that afternoon at two o'clock.

When Blair and Flurry got to the Senate and reported

Eastland's suggestion, Kefauver gave his assent and promised to be there. Leaving the chamber, Blair stopped long enough to call Collins and tell him to go ahead as planned. Then, since it was almost one-thirty, he and Flurry hurried over to the Senate cafeteria and, after a long wait in line, finally got their lunch. By the time they got back to the Judiciary conference room, it was just past two. When they hurried in, they found no senators present but Collins, Chumbris, Raitt, Sonosky, Ellenbogen, and, to their astonishment, both Cutler and Foley. Figuring that the industry men must be there by prearrangement, Blair and Flurry sat down and began arranging their papers. As they did, the conversation, which had broken off abruptly when they came in, resumed, but now it was rather strained and desultory. Finally, after a few minutes, Blair turned to Collins and asked, "Where are all the senators?" Collins inquired whether he'd got his message, and Blair replied that he'd been too busy to return to his office or even to call in. At this, Collins explained that Mansfield had refused to go along with Eastland's plan, so the meeting had been canceled, as he had informed both Kefauver's and Blair's secretaries.

Blair and Flurry suddenly realized that they had stumbled on another secret meeting. They sat tight, and finally the conference got under way again—slowly and awkwardly, to be sure, but in time everyone became resigned to the presence of Kefauver's men, and the discussion ultimately got to be fairly normal. Afterward, Collins, apparently aware that he now couldn't exclude the two men, invited them to join in the rest of their deliberations. Later, Eastland decided that he wasn't anxious to have the administration disclaim responsibility for participating, so he asked for someone with more authority than Sonosky, and the administration sent over its Deputy Attorney-General, Nicholas Katzenbach. Toward the end, the drug industry also sent in its first-stringer—Thomas Corcoran (better known as Tommy the Cork), who had been one of the chief architects of the New Deal; now a private, and highly successful, lawyer, he was generally considered to be extremely adept at presenting a persuasive argument at the right time.

During this period, the thalidomide story had receded, and therefore the industry's resistance to the new amendments had stiffened. Of all the arguments that ensued, one of the bitterest concerned the evidence required to establish a drug's efficacy. Cutler insisted that the law should require only "substantial" evidence, while Sonosky held out for "preponderant" evidence. As Sonosky saw it, if a hundred doctors tested the drug and only twenty considered it effective, for all juridical purposes the twenty could present "substantial" proof of efficacy whereas "preponderant" meant that a sizable majority of those testing the drug would have to find it effective before it could be approved. To everyone's surprise, including their own, Blair and Cutler turned out to be on the same side in this instance. Blair said that since, generally speaking, any innovation was apt to meet with opposition, he was willing to accept "substantial" evidence, but he insisted that the amendment stipulate that the evidence consist of "adequate and well-controlled investigations, including clinical investigations, by experts qualified by scientific training and experience to evaluate the effectiveness of the drug involved." Cutler docilely went along with this, astonishing Sonosky. "I just couldn't believe it when Blair pulled that off," he said later. "It gives us all

kinds of power—especially the word 'adequat
sure that drugs do what is claimed for them."

On August 11th, Mansfield moved to cut off the
then in its sixth day, by filing a cloture petition—a
mentary device, requiring a two-thirds majority, that h
been used successfully for thirty-five years. During that period, senators who backed civil-rights legislation had tried using cloture petitions eleven times, without success. The welfare of private industry was evidently far less controversial than the welfare of private citizens, for on August 14th the cloture motion passed easily, and a couple of days later so did the satellite bill. (Subsequently, the President appointed Merck's Connor to the corporation's board, and then Cutler was named to handle the incorporating work.)

After the bill passed, two of the filibusterers—Douglas and Russell Long, of Louisiana—got up and delivered an eighteenth-century epigram:

LONG: The law locks up
DOUGLAS: Both man and woman
LONG: Who steal the goose
DOUGLAS: From off the common,
LONG: But lets the greater felon loose
DOUGLAS: Who steals the common from the goose.

On August 20th, the members of the Judiciary Committee held their last meeting to consider the President's amendments, and, having approved them, voted out the fourth version of S. 1552 unanimously. Immeasurably stronger than the Eastland-Dirksen bill, it called for strict factory inspection; improved standards of quality controls in manufacturing; the abolition of automatic approval of new-drug applications after a fixed period; proof of efficacy in all new drugs and old drugs; the rejection of new-drug applications and the withdrawal of approved drugs in cases of false labeling; the use on all labels and in all advertising and promotional material of generic names in letters at least half as large as the trade names; a requirement that the Secretary of Health, Education, and Welfare review all existing generic names and establish new and simpler ones where they were needed; distribution by the F.D.A. of package inserts to all doctors, hospitals, and medical facilities; the keeping of records by drug companies on the side effects of all their drugs; the certification of all antibiotics; and descriptions in all drug advertising of a drug's efficacy and adverse side effects. About all that remained of the Eastland-Dirksen bill was the stipulation that the Patent Office had the right to ask for information on drugs from the F.D.A. and the provision that the name and address of every pharmaceutical company be listed with the government.

When the meeting broke up, Kefauver was first out of the room. "This is a very good drug bill," he told a group of reporters waiting outside. "I think it will give a great deal of added protection to the American people."

XIII

As a deliberative body, the Senate does most of its deliberating out of the public eye, and by the time a measure reaches the floor, its general outline is largely set. Members who are unfamiliar with a bill's contents are likely to follow their party leader or a colleague who holds similar views and has a constituency like theirs. Since S. 1552 had not only the unanimous support of the committee having jurisdiction over it but the backing of the administration and the public, there was little doubt that it would pass much as it stood. Now that it was no longer controversial, Kefauver's colleagues, most of whom had avoided taking a stand on the bill earlier, began calling his office for material to use in speeches praising the measure. The only contention anticipated was over the compulsory-licensing provision, which Kefauver intended to submit as an amendment. But even this was not expected to stir up much debate. Nor was it thought to have any chance of going through. The general opinion was that it would get eight or possibly ten votes at the most.

At 11 A.M. on August 23rd, the Senate took up S. 1552. First, Eastland outlined the bill's legislative history; that is, the intent of Congress as it is expressed in the views of a bill's supporters, which later helps the courts interpret the law. He read a lengthy description of what S. 1552 set out to do and how it meant to do it, and when he had finished and headed for the cloakroom, cigar in hand, Kefauver got up to retrace some of the steps, fill in a few missing points, and object to certain parts of the bill, which he felt had been weakened in committee. As usual, he was not audible more than a dozen feet away, so Hruska and Keating, the only senators who stayed in the chamber throughout his speech, moved over to the Democratic side of the aisle to hear him better. After Kefauver sat down, both Keating and Hruska spoke up for the bill, which they had both voted against a few weeks earlier, and Hruska brought up the question of compulsory licensing before Kefauver could. "To charge that prices are too high and to promise a reduction by legislation leads many a demagogue politician into a wonderful dream world," he stated. "Sometimes it goes so far that he even convinces himself of his own virtue and prowess as a 'friend and deliverer of the people.'"

Then Dirksen rose and, addressing the presiding officer, said, "Mr. President, in all of this effort I have been pretty well excoriated in the press. I do not whimper. It does not make any difference to me. I have a responsibility and I try to articulate it under my oath as best I can. I am a little proud of a record that goes pretty far back, Mr. President, as I think of my own conduct as a public servant. . . . The old Irish [*sic*] poet of long ago, John Donne, said, 'Every man's death diminishes me for I am a part of mankind.' Mr. President, I am of mankind. May that sentiment, that feeling, and that impulse never forsake me when I undertake to sit with my senatorial colleagues . . . in the hope that we can derive something feasible, workable, and in the interest of the whole country, and in particular the consumer."

When the Senate finally got down to business, Kefauver and Humphrey offered an amendment requiring that all prescription drugs be tested on animals before being used on human beings, which was accepted by unanimous consent. Then Javits, who had learned from the Library of Congress following the Dr. Kelsey hearings that not a single state required physicians to tell their patients that they were taking experimental drugs, proposed an amendment making it mandatory for a doctor to get a patient's permission before treating him with a drug that the F.D.A. had not yet approved. Although the suggestion appeared sound enough, just about everyone except Carroll and Javits himself was against it. Kefauver was, for one, because he feared that the A.M.A. would consider the amendment an infringement of the physician's rights, and would oppose it; the A.M.A. can always muster considerable force, and he felt that if it moved into action, it might bring down the entire bill. He also pointed out, as did several other senators, the problem that a physician would face in getting such permission from someone who was in the terminal stage of an illness but was not aware of it, or from someone who was unconscious. Javits and Kefauver had a long conference, from which Javits came away convinced that some sort of compromise was necessary.

Around that time, in the corridor behind the Senate gallery, Ellenbogen, who was standing by to offer technical assistance, showed Sonosky a copy of a press release that H.E.W. had put out that morning. "Tablets of thalidomide, unidentified by name and which may be mistaken for other drugs, are still at large in family medicine cabinets," it began, and went on to say that the manufacturer (Merrell) had distributed 2,528,412 thalidomide tablets, in a variety of colors and sizes, to twelve hundred and sixty-seven doctors, who had given them to some twenty thousand patients, in containers that bore nothing more than directions for use. The F.D.A. had been unable to track down ninety-nine of the physicians, the release said, and of the rest four hundred and ten had made no effort to get in touch with the patients to whom they had given thalidomide—in many cases because they had kept no record of doing so. The F.D.A., the release continued, had no idea how many tablets were still around. Most of the doctors had received the manufacturer's warning to stop using the drug in March, 1962, but eighty-five of them said they had not been notified of the product's side effects, and forty-two others said that they had received no warning at all. The F.D.A. had asked the doctors whether they had signed statements that they were qualified to test the drug; six hundred and forty had said they had, two hundred and forty-seven had said they had not, and the rest couldn't remember or didn't answer the question.

When Sonosky finished reading the release, he asked Ellenbogen to have the department send twenty copies of it to the Senate press gallery at once. Then he hurried off to look for Eastland. He finally found him in the Senate reception room, just outside the chamber, talking to Cutler. Sonosky handed the Senator the release. After glancing through it, Eastland said, "That does it, gentlemen!" Handing the release to Cutler, he returned to the Senate chamber.

By that time, Javits was ready with a modified amendment, stating simply that "the interests of patients" should be considered when the Secretary of Health, Education, and Welfare issued regulations to cover the use of experimental drugs. Although the provision was weaker than Javits liked, he and most of the other senators felt that it would, in effect, put doctors on notice that malpractice suits over the use of experimental drugs would now be more likely to be sustained by the courts. A voice vote was taken, and the modified amendment passed unanimously.

The only remaining matter to be considered was Kefauver's old compulsory-licensing provision, which had fared so badly in committee. Before he got up to propose restoring it to the bill, Blair, who was standing nearby, had a brief, whispered conversation with him. The night before, Blair had worked late, and as he left his office and headed for the elevator, he heard Kefauver's voice booming down the corridor. Never having heard the Senator raise his voice above a mumble, Blair hurried to Kefauver's office, only to find that he was merely talking to a friend on a long-distance wire, and, like many people his age, seemed to feel that he had to shout to get through. Recalling this, Blair leaned over and said, "When you get up there, Estes, just imagine that you're talking on the telephone to a deaf old lady in a small town in Tennessee over a bad connection."

When Kefauver got the floor, he apparently took the advice; in any case, he spoke, for once, loudly and clearly. This was fortunate, for close to fifty senators were in the chamber, milling about and chatting in small groups, and within a matter of seconds they had quieted down to listen. One of them explained his interest by saying, "First of all, I'd never heard Estes make so much noise, and, second, I knew that this was the heart of his whole fight for lower prices." To a number of those on hand, the amendment that Kefauver offered was something of a surprise, for it was not his original proposal—that after three years a patent holder would be obliged to license any qualified applicant at a royalty rate of up to eight per cent. Instead, he now moved that a patent holder be obliged to license any qualified applicant, up to the same royalty rate, on any drug that the F.T.C. found to be selling for more than five hundred per cent of its production cost—including the cost of materials, labor, royalties, and research.

Blair had set up several charts on metal easels at the rear of the chamber, and now Kefauver moved over to one of them, which showed price figures for prednisone. After explaining that the patent on the substance was being contested in the Patent Office by five large companies and that for the time being any firm could produce and sell it, Kefauver pointed out that several of the companies that claimed to have discovered it—Schering, Merck, and others—sold it to druggists at precisely $170 per thousand tablets, although according to an estimate drawn up by the subcommittee staff it cost these companies no more than $13.61 to produce and package a thousand tablets. McKesson & Robbins, however, he went on, holding up a bottle of prednisone, had also been selling the drug and had informed him that its costs were $8.99 a thousand tablets and that it sold a thousand to druggists for $20.95. "If any one of these large companies gets the patent, it will only license other large companies," Kefauver said. "The arthritics and old people will be denied the right to buy prednisone made by McKesson & Robbins . . . at two or three cents a tablet. They will have to pay nearly thirty cents a tablet, as they do now when they buy prednisone under a trade name."

Senator Frank J. Lausche, a conservative Democrat from Ohio, got to his feet and stared at the chart in disbelief for several minutes. Finally, he turned to Kefauver and asked, "Is there any dispute about the fact the Senator from Tennesee has just pointed out?"

Kefauver assured him that there wasn't, and Lausche sat down again.

A moment later, Senator Jack Miller, a Republican from Iowa, rose and said, "This does not concern me very much, because it seems to me that if the product is the same and there is such a differential in price, people naturally will buy the twenty-dollar bottle of pills instead of the hundred-and-seventy-dollar bottle of pills."

Kefauver replied that if a doctor wrote, say, "Meticorten" (Schering's trade name for prednisone) on a prescription blank for an arthritic patient, the patient had to buy Meticorten or nothing. Miller resumed his seat.

Another antagonist was Eastland, who had been conferring with Hruska and Dirksen. "The Senator is not going to put a noose around the drug industry's neck and still get research!" he shouted.

"Let me say that it is a little farfetched to take the position that a drug company could not get along with a markup of five hundred per cent on its production costs," Kefauver said, "including its costs of research, when no other industry has markups that high. Furthermore, an eight-per-cent royalty would be paid." Then, turning to another chart, he read off a list of major drugs that had been discovered abroad and were being sold here by licensees. Fifty pills of chlorpromazine, he noted, were sold by Rhône-Poulenc, its discoverer, in France for fifty-one cents and by Smith, Kline & French in the United States for $3.03, while a hundred pills of reserpine were sold by CIBA in Germany for $1.05 and by its subsidiary here for $4.50, and fifty pills of tolbutamide were sold in Germany by Hoechst for $1.85 and by Upjohn here for $4.17. After pointing out that the research for all these drugs had been done abroad, Kefauver said, "Mr. President, that is not right."

Again Lausche got up and stared at the chart. After a moment, he asked what explanation Smith, Kline & French had given of the price they charged for chlorpromazine.

Kefauver turned to still another chart, which showed drug-company profits. Pointing out the Smith, Kline & French data, he said, "[Their net profit] after taxes was twenty-two and seven-tenths per cent, up until 1954, when Thorazine [the trade name for chlorpromazine] was introduced. As the Senator knows, it is a very potent tranquillizer. After taxes, the net profit on investment [that year] was thirty-seven per cent. It reached up to fifty per cent in 1955. In other words, that rate of profit would almost pay for the company in two years."

Throughout these exchanges, Senator John O. Pastore, a Democrat from Rhode Island, had been pacing near his desk, in the front row. Since he had led the fight for the satellite bill, the general assumption was that it would be a long time before he went to Kefauver's aid. Now he asked Kefauver, "Would any of the evidence which was adduced before the subcommittee indicate that drugs developed in the United States are sold at higher prices to Americans [than] to persons who live in other countries?"

Kefauver assured him that there was indeed evidence of this, and that, in fact, some of the drugs that sold more cheaply abroad were not only developed but manufactured here.

Hruska rose and asked, "Is it not true that in most European countries there are price-fixing statutes which control the prices of drugs?"

This question suggested not only that other countries had seen fit to limit runaway drug prices but that American firms were able to sell abroad at a profit even so.

Pastore was quivering with indignation. Facing the chamber, he cried, "I say it is immoral!"

Kefauver nodded. "It is immoral," he said quietly. "There is no doubt about it."

A few minutes later, to Kefauver's surprise, Mansfield moved simply to table the patent-licensing amendment—a motion that, under the Senate's rules, is not subject to debate.

Kefauver hurried over to Mansfield's desk. "Hell, Mike, if anybody's going to do that, let it be Dirksen," he said. "Why not let us vote on the merits of it?"

Mansfield dismissed the suggestion, explaining that the White House had instructed him to make the motion. A buzzer rang twice, for a quorum call, and as soon as enough members had assembled, it rang three times, for a vote. Fifty-three senators voted in favor of Mansfield's motion. Twenty-eight—three times as many as Kefauver had expected—voted against it. Of the latter, all but one (Margaret Chase Smith, of Maine) were Democrats. Even Humphrey voted with Kefauver. "I hate to go against the leadership," he told a colleague at the time, adding, with a nod toward the charts, "but, my God, you can't ignore those." According to several other senators, the amendment would have got far more votes—perhaps enough to win—if the administration had not implicitly opposed it.

Shortly before seven that evening, a roll-call vote was taken on the entire bill. It was seventy-eight to nothing in favor.

Afterward, Senator Douglas rose to praise Kefauver for his efforts, and while he spoke, Kefauver sat with downcast eyes, looking rather embarrassed. "The Senator from Tennessee has waged a long and lonely fight for an adequate drug bill," Douglas said. "He has been attacked by the powerful drug industry, and . . . he has not received a great deal of coöperation from some of his colleagues. . . . But now, Mr. President, because of the many terrible tragedies which have occurred in European countries from the use of the drug thalidomide and the cases which have occurred in this country, it has been proved that the Senator was right all the time. . . . Men who had openly and secretly fought him now flock to get on the bandwagon and pretend that they were always his supporters. As a humble American citizen, I wish to commend the Senator from Tennessee, and all those who helped him, for fighting all these months and years for this great reform. Certainly, the American people will eternally be grateful to him. Mr. President, can we learn from this lesson, or can mankind educate itself only by disaster and tragedy?"

When Douglas resumed his seat, Blair turned to Kefauver,

and said, "I remember one spring day back in 1948 when I was up in the gallery here, watching a debate. I saw you come into the chamber through the rear door and stand there, looking around. You had just started your campaign for the Senate, and I figured that you had used your floor privileges as a member of the House to see what it was like over here, and what you were fighting for. Well, Estes, this is that you came here for."

Looking even more embarrassed, Kefauver didn't answer. Then, after a time, he pursed his lips several times and nodded, almost imperceptibly.

XIV

All reports indicated that there would be a lengthy delay before the House got around to considering the drug bill, and now that the thalidomide story was no longer front-page news, Kefauver was worried that the industry might move in again and start chipping away at the bill. However, several Washington reporters—most notably Miriam Ottenberg, a Pulitzer Prize-winning writer on the *Evening Star*—wrote a number of stories that helped keep the drug issue alive.

A few days after the Senate passed S. 1552, Miss Ottenberg wrote about another Merrell drug, MER/29, which had been widely sold for the previous year and a half as an anti-cholesterol preparation. According to the article, Merrell had submitted a new-drug application to the F.D.A. on MER/29 in July of 1959. Before the doctor in the F.D.A.'s New Drug Division who was assigned to it had gone very far, he resigned to go into private practice, and the application was turned over to a new employee—"Dr. X," Miss Ottenberg called him—who had just completed his residency. Dissatisfied with the file on the drug, he nonetheless could find nothing specific, under the law, to object to, and finally approved it. "The American Medical Association convention was coming up, and they [the Merrell people] were anxious to promote the drug," he told her. "I was getting daily telephone calls."

Six months later, reports began to reach the F.D.A. indicating that MER/29 appeared to have some side effects; a Mayo Clinic bulletin stated that it seemed to make hair fall out and skin peel, and, a little later, a professor of medicine informed Dr. X that he had produced cataracts in rats with the substance. Dr. X called both of these reports to the company's attention, and was assured that they would be looked into. Subsequently, he went to his superiors and recommended that MER/29 be taken off the market at once. The F.D.A.'s legal staff was consulted, and it said that the agency had no power to take such an action; once a drug was approved, it stayed approved. Then, shortly afterward, in September, 1961, Dr. X followed his predecessor into private practice. The problem he left behind grew rapidly. By the end of October, the F.D.A. was convinced that MER/29 was exceedingly toxic; in fact, the evidence that its investigators had collected indicated that, in addition to the side effects that had shown up earlier, the drug could cause diminished hormone production, impotence, liver damage, and cataracts in humans.

The F.D.A.'s only recourse was to try to persuade Merrell to remove the drug voluntarily. At the time that the agency was discussing this with the company, a two-page advertisement for MER/29 appeared in the *Journal* of the American Medical Association, which stated, "We know that, after use in more than 300,000 patients, few toxic or serious side effects have been reported, thus tending to reaffirm the safety margins previously established." A few days later, the F.D.A. appealed to H.E.W.'s general counsel, which also reported that under existing law the government was powerless.

Five months later, Merrell suddenly took the drug off the market. Afterward, a high official of the F.D.A. stated publicly that MER/29 should never have been approved in the first place. However, it turned out that the F.D.A. had not been entirely at fault. Shortly before Merrell withdrew the drug, the F.D.A. got tipped off that the company had allegedly not submitted all the results of its clinical tests. A team of F.D.A. inspectors paid a surprise visit to the company and, according to an F.D.A. report, "data on monkeys was obtained which differed from that submitted in the original new-drug application in support of the safety of MER/29." Later, the Justice Department turned the case over to a federal grand jury, which brought in an indictment against the firm. The case has yet to be tried.

Shortly afterward, Miss Ottenberg described the case history of a clinical investigator called "Dr. Z," who had tested a wide variety of different drugs for a dozen pharmaceutical companies, and had then written articles praising them unstintingly for eight different medical journals. Although Dr. Z was only thirty-one years old and had behind him one year of internship and no residency, he had convinced the companies concerned, all of which he had approached first, that he was qualified to test their products on such ailments as infant dysentery, pregnancy disorders, pneumonia, postoperative difficulties, stomach trouble, and bronchitis. Besides whatever fees his patients paid, the companies paid him ten to fifteen dollars for every patient tested. On the average, he received two thousand dollars for each drug that he checked out. (Not long before this article of Miss Ottenberg's appeared, the F.D.A. had announced that it had quite a few cases of rigged research on file. These fell into two main categories—doctors who were paid by pharmaceutical houses to test new drugs and who either altered the results or did no testing whatever, in either case submitting favorable reports; and what the F.D.A. called "research quacks," doctors who made a few uncontrolled observations on a handful of patients and then submitted their records as clinical evidence. According to one university research physician quoted in the *Wall Street Journal,* "I know personally three cases of doctors whose services are for sale. They are told what a drug is supposed to do, and they promptly prove it." Moreover, he added, some drug companies went so far as to design the "clinical" experiments, write the testing physicians' reports, and then pay him for the use of his name.)

A week later, Miss Ottenberg described a manual put out by Merrell shortly after it had submitted its new-drug application on thalidomide. Entitled "The Kevadon Hospital Clinical Program," it outlined the company's forthcoming campaign on the drug, which was to be initiated at a conference of twenty-one division managers, eight hospital representatives, and sixteen selected salesmen. "The program is geared to establish, during the next two months or so, approximately 800 established studies, averaging 20 patients per study," the manual stated. "Your principal sources of contact will be in the general teaching hospital. . . . This program is designed to gain widespread confirmation of [Kevadon's] usefulness in a variety of hospitalized patients. If your work yields case reports, personal communications or published work, all well and good. But the main purpose is to establish local studies whose results will be spread among hospital staff members. . . . Appeal to the doctor's ego—we think he is important enough to be selected as one of the first to use Kevadon in that section of the country." Under "A Word of Caution," the manual added, "Bear in mind that these are not basic clinical research studies. We have firmly established the safety, dosage and usefulness of Kevadon by both foreign and U.S. laboratory and clinical studies."

XV

On the day the Senate approved S. 1552, the House Committee on Interstate and Foreign Commerce completed its hearings on the Harris bill. The chairman, Oren Harris, who had represented the Fourth District of Arkansas for twenty-two years, was generally considered one of the ablest men in the House and also one of the business world's staunchest allies. In his committee, which was made up of twenty Democrats—eight of them Southerners—and thirteen Republicans, the conservatives of both parties had a two-to-one margin of control. The administration could have bypassed Harris, it was pointed out, simply by sending S. 1552 over to the House after it passed the Senate, but the President was apparently unwilling to do so. Those who had pressed for a strong bill thought the chances of getting one were slim, though just about everyone was confident that some kind of bill would go through. "Harris knows there's no way to stop a drug bill from being passed," one of his committee colleagues remarked. "The people demand it, and the White House has gone along with them. It's too loaded to fight." Besides, Celler was lurking in the wings with his bill, and it seemed likely that if Harris failed to move, the members of Celler's committee might decide to yield to public pressure and then reap the applause.

Perhaps the most compelling reason for believing that a drug bill would be enacted in that session, though, was that opposition within the industry had weakened. Since March, the value of shares in the twenty-two largest pharmaceutical companies studied during the drug hearings had fallen anywhere from ten per cent to a much as sixty per cent, with an average drop of about a third. Surveys showed that people were reducing their consumption of drugs; even sales of aspirin had dropped. Some elements within the industry actually wanted a bill—though not a strong bill—to help assure consumers about the safety of drugs.

Kefauver assumed that now that the White House was behind the drug bill, it would make its own contacts in the House to see to it that the bill coming out of the Harris committee would either be the same as S. 1552 or very much like it. However, around the 1st of September, he learned that two of the strongest liberal Democrats on the Harris committee—John D. Dingell, of Michigan, and John E. Moss, of California, had still not heard from anyone in the executive branch. Kefauver asked Blair to see what he could do, and Blair called Deputy Attorney-General Katzenbach. After reporting what Kefauver had learned, Blair added that he himself had seen a lengthy list of changes that the P.M.A. hoped to incorporate in the Harris bill, and asked him to let Dingell and Moss know that the administration preferred S. 1552. Katzenbach promised to call them. Dingell and Moss have yet to hear from him.

In fact, it wasn't until September 13th, twenty-one days after S. 1552 passed the Senate, that the administration made any approach to the Harris committee. On that day, Sonosky met with Dingell and Moss to discuss the drug bill's prospects. Because the two congressmen were far too busy at the time with end-of-the-session matters to familiarize themselves with the Senate measure, both believed the Harris bill to be the stronger; in fact, Moss was under the impression that S. 1552 was the Eastland-Dirksen bill. Sonosky did not try to persuade them otherwise. Indeed, when Moss asked him whether the administration preferred S. 1552 or the Harris bill, he replied that they were both acceptable. "It's not my business to tell members of Congress how to vote," he explained later.

When Kefauver heard about this, he picked up his telephone and called Feldman's office, only to be informed by a secretary there that he was in a conference and wouldn't be able to return his call until the next day. Since the Harris committee was scheduled to meet at ten o'clock the following morning, Kefauver told her that his business was urgent, and asked her to have Feldman call him at home that evening. However, it was noon the next day before Feldman called back. By then, it was too late, for word had just come through that the Harris committee had begun to vote on its bill.

The drug lobbyists had remained quite inconspicuous during the committee proceedings in the Senate, but it appeared that they considered members of the House more approachable, for when the Harris committee members got to the door of the conference room on the morning of September 19th, they found twenty industry men on hand. Among them were two former congressmen—Joseph P. O'Hara, who had been the second-ranking Republican on the Harris committee and now was in private law practice in Washington, and Harry L. Towe, who was now secretary and general counsel for Medical Economics, one of the country's largest medical publishing houses. Off to one side, the members of the general staff—Foley, Cutler, and Corcoran—were conferring.

According to a lobbyist for one of the large drug firms, Cutler had done a masterly job on the Senate side but had been somewhat inattentive to the ins and outs of procedure in the House. "The one big error he made was that just before the Harris committee met he handed each member a fifty-page rewrite of the bill to bring it in line with what the P.M.A. wanted," the man explained. "Congressmen simply don't have the time or the staff help to get through a document like that. The way we ordinarily do it is to type up amendments—a sentence here, a paragraph there—on separate pieces of paper. We parcel them out among the different congressmen who are friendly toward us, and when the time comes, it's a simple matter for them to take the slips out of their pockets and offer them." As it happened, the P.M.A. rewrite was essentially identical with the Eastland-Dirksen bill.

Moss and Dingell, who had by now had a chance to study S. 1552 and had found it much stronger than they expected, hoped to substitute it for the Harris bill, but at that first meeting of the committee they found that so many of the other liberals had already gone home to campaign that the votes simply weren't there. In time, though, they also found that Harris was fighting most of the P.M.A. amendments. He had promised the White House to bring the bill pretty much in line with S. 1552, it was reported—a report leading to more speculation about why the administration hadn't sent the Senate bill intact to the House. During the first meeting, the committee adopted the Senate amendment on efficacy and strengthened the amendments on quality controls and experimental-drug testing, going as far as to require the consent of the patient in the latter.

But it was touch-and-go on every point, for the drug industry had a number of friends on the committee. Dingell was outraged by attempts to weaken the bill and, particularly, by the P.M.A.'s proposed revision. As he came out of the first meeting at lunchtime, he ran into Sonosky and Cutler in the hall and stopped for a moment. "I'm sick and tired of these pharmaceutical people," he said to Sonosky. "They accepted something in the Senate, and now they come over here and welsh on it. If this goes on, I'm going to be forced to compile a dossier on what's happened and make a speech about it on the floor."

At seven o'clock on the evening of September 21st, the Harris committee reported out its bill. Dingell told a reporter at the time that it was much stronger than he had expected, explaining, "The chairman fought hard and did a real public service," but he added, "Still, the results fell far short of what I would have liked."

In Kefauver's view, the House measure was woefully inadequate. Although the efficacy amendent and the amendments on quality controls and drug testing had been strengthened along lines that he approved of, and so had the provision on factory inspection, his amendments on registration of all manufacturers with the government, on animal testing, on F.D.A. consultation with the Patent Office, on the certification of antibiotics used in animal feed, and on the distribution of package inserts to all physicians had been dropped. Worst of all, the committee had adopted the S. 1552 advertising amendment and then rendered it ineffective by adding a clause stating that it didn't apply as long as advertisements carried a note informing the reader that a full description of the drug, including its side effects, could be obtained by writing to the manufacturer.

According to the Pink Sheet, "The biggest job of all was done by former Rep. Harry Towe, a NJ GOP-er, who represented Medical Economics and was credited with the House cmte. language taking Rx drug advertising off the Senate hook." However that may be, the job was done in the time-tested fashion; that is, a one-paragraph amendment was given to a sympathetic congressman—in this case, J. Arthur Younger, a Republican from California—and he distributed copies of it to his colleagues. As for Harris, though he opposed the P.M.A. on most of what it wanted, he supported it on this amendment.

XVI

Back in early August, Sonosky had included the advertising provision from the original S. 1552 in the so-called President's bill at the risk of incurring a good deal of displeasure, in H.E.W. and out. He strongly believed in the importance of the amendment, and now that it had been lost, he was determined to have it restored in the House, so he called Cohen that same night to suggest that they take the fight to the floor. Cohen promised to think about it, and the following Monday morning he told Sonosky that he had talked the suggestion over with Feldman and that the White House had given the project its blessing. The next step, Cohen added, was to find the man to lead the fight. Sonosky at once suggested Congressman John A. Blatnik, the Minnesota Democrat who had conducted hearings on false and misleading advertising of tranquillizers back in 1958. At that time, Sonosky, who was a Minnesotan himself, had served as associate counsel on Blatnik's Subcommittee on Legal and Monetary Affairs. As he pointed out to Cohen, Blatnik, in addition to being more familiar with the subject of drug advertising than anyone else in the House, had almost perfect qualifications. For one thing, he was chairman of the Rivers and Harbors Subcommittee of the House Committee on Public Works, one of the chief sources of pork-barrel funds, which no congressman can ignore. And, for another, he was widely respected as a hard-working, level-headed liberal.

While Sonosky and Cohen were planning their strategy, Dingell decided independently to fight the new advertising amendment on the floor, and got in touch with Kefauver to ask his help. Kefauver said Blair would do anything he could, and Dingell was just preparing to round up fellow-members whom he thought he could count on when his telephone rang. It was Sonosky, to tell him about the new plan and ask for his coöperation. Dingell called Blair to find out how Kefauver would feel about this, and was told that the Senator would be glad to help out. Actually, Kefauver had already done so, having got in touch with Feldman, Speaker of the House John W. McCormack, and House Majority Leader Carl Albert about the advertising amendment, and having extracted from each of them a promise to support it.

On Monday, September 24th, Sonosky asked Blatnik whether he was interested in managing things on the floor. Blatnik said he was, and early the next morning he began rounding up support among fellow-congressmen, the Democratic Study Group, an aggregation of a hundred and twenty-five liberal congressmen, of which he was the head, and the

A.F.L.-C.I.O. Committee on Health Legislation. Then, from three o'clock that afternoon until seven that evening, Blatnik, Dingell, Blair, Sonosky, and Stuart H. Johnson, Jr., the chief counsel for Celler's committee (Celler had been summoned home because his wife was ill) met in Dingell's office to map their strategy.

The following day, a number of things happened. Various staff members began whipping up two- and three-minute speeches citing examples of misleading advertising, which several representatives were to deliver. A letter arrived for Blatnik from Secretary Celebrezze, strongly supporting his move to eliminate the Younger amendment. Blatnik forwarded the letter to Dingell, whose office had become the group's command center, and a large number of copies were made. At Dingell's request, Blair wrote a letter on the evils of the Younger amendment, which was signed by Dingell, Blatnik, and half a dozen other interested congressmen and was copied to be distributed through the House, along with Celebrezze's letter. Dingell called several friendly reporters and asked them for some coverage in the next morning's papers, so that congressmen could read of the fight at breakfast. (The Washington *Post* ran a seven-column news story, under the heading "Celebrezze Joins Fight Against Drug Bill Loophole," and an editorial that concluded, "A simple matter of truthful labeling is involved in an area where a mistake can have tragic results. The House ought to restore the language proposed by President Kennedy to the drug bill.")

Shortly after Blair had completed his letter and sent it off to Dingell's office by messenger, a drug-industry lawyer with whom he was on fairly good terms called and wanted to know what the House was up to. Replying that he hadn't the least idea, Blair told him that Kefauver was furious about the way the industry had reneged on the Senate bill. The man replied that he had informed Sonosky about their intentions of fighting the Senate amendments in the House. "Sonosky is not a member of the Subcommittee on Antitrust and Monopoly," Blair said. "He didn't tell us." When he hung up, Blair leaned back in his chair, and grinned. "They're scared!" he said. "They didn't expect us to fight this, and they don't know *how* we're going to fight it. I'll bet they're terrified that Estes will get up and give another hell-raising speech."

Around five o'clock in the afternoon, Dingell hurried over to the House chamber for a roll-call vote, and when he got back, he telephoned Sonosky, and said, "Boy, I don't know what you've been doing, but they're on the run!" he said. "They're caving in all over the place!" Younger had disowned his own amendment, Dingell went on, and Sonosky interrupted to explain how this had come about. As it happened, Younger was conducting a campaign for reëlection out in San Mateo County, California, and someone had relayed the facts on his amendment to his opponent, William Keller, with the result that Keller had been using the information in his speeches, which were receiving a big play by the press. "If he's as scared as all that, we've got it made," Dingell said. He felt that they ought to get together wtih Younger and work out some kind of compromise, though, he went on, adding, "There's no point in chopping him up on the floor if we don't have to."

However, if Younger appeared to be on the run that night, he was standing stock-still the next morning and looked as if he meant to hold fast. The House convened at noon that day, and an hour later the Harris bill came up for debate, under a three-hour limit set by the Rules Committee. (Such time limits apply only to actual debate.) Harris was allotted half the time, and the ranking Republican on the committee, John B. Bennett, of Michigan, was given the other half. They then doled it out to members of their parties. Harris used part of his time to describe H.R. 11581 point by point. "This bill is very much in the public interest," he concluded. Representative Bennett spoke next, taking issue with a number of provisions—mainly for the record, it appeared, because in the end he said, "I shall vote for the bill, and I hope it will pass."

Ordinarily, what is said about a bill on the floor of the House has little effect on its fate; speeches are made for the record, usually by congressmen who feel that they need to justify their vote. Far more important than speeches are quick, whispered agreements made by groups of two or three men, on the floor and off. Throughout the early speeches, Dingell and Blatnik were busy lining up support, and so were the drug-industry lobbyists. Corcoran, Foley, and Cutler were sitting in a row in the gallery. Most of the time, they listened to the proceedings, but now and then one of them whispered something to the others and left for a few minutes. Most noticeable among the lobbyists were Towe and O'Hara, who, as former congressmen, had floor privileges, and who did not hesitate to use them. At one point, Dingell turned to a colleague and said, "Look at those two! They're covering this place like a carpet!" Sonosky and a couple of his co-workers from Health, Education, and Welfare were buttonholing congressmen in the corridors and anterooms, and so were Kenneth Meiklejohn and John Curran, two representatives of the A.F.L.-C.I.O.

At a little before three o'clock, Dingell was given the

floor, and he proceeded to insert in the record a couple of cases of misleading advertising from the Senate subcommittee's hearings. The first dealt with claims made for Pfizer's oral antidiabetic, Diabinese—those that had ignored evidence submitted by the company's own clinical investigator to its president showing that the drug had a twenty-seven-per-cent incidence of side effects. The second case concerned Medrol, a cortical steroid sold by Upjohn for the treatment of a wide variety of ailments. According to one advertisement, embellished with what appeared to be before-and-after X-rays, Medrol was highly effective in the treatment of ulcerative colitis. Dingell, displaying enlarged photostats of the X-rays, pointed out that the X-rays were of two different people, neither of whom had taken Medrol. In conclusion, he quoted an A.M.A. study, which had found that "perhaps the largest source of information to practitioners was the advertisements they received in the several medical journals."

At a little before four o'clock, by which time around two hundred congressmen were present, the Clerk of the House began reading the bill, and Blatnik, who had been busy behind the scenes most of the day, telephoned William Phillips, the staff director of the Democratic Study Group, and told him to make the first of two whip calls. Phillips and his staff at once telephoned four regional whips, each of whom called six others, and then all twenty-four called from four to six members apiece. Within twelve minutes, every available member of the group had been asked to hurry to the floor for a vote. Half an hour later, Blatnik got to the floor to offer his amendment, which merely erased Younger's.

In the end, Blatnik's speech was more effective that the work of all the lobbyists put together. Like Dingell, he cited several deceptive drug advertisements, but far more important was his simple repetition, at several points, of the phrase "the Younger amendment;" each time the words were spoken, Younger flinched, and glanced up at the press gallery, where a couple of dozen reporters were taking notes. Then, when Blatnik had finished his speech, Younger got up, unhesitatingly denied that the amendment was his, and added, "Therefore, I have no objection whatsoever to the amendment which the gentleman from Minnesota offers." (Later that day, Younger asked Blatnik to edit his name out of the record, because of the trouble he was having back home, and Blatnik obliged him to the extent of eliminating all but one reference. A few weeks later, Younger was reëlected by the largest margin he had had in six contests.)

Normally, when the sponsor of an amendment disowns it, that is the end of it. In this instance, however, to everyone's surprise, Harris jumped up and objected to Younger's retraction. It is most uncommon for a member of Congress to back down as Younger had without first informing his committee chairman, so that he can retrench all around. But Younger, in his haste to get out of a tight corner, had neglected to inform Harris. Harris afterward admitted that he was put out by what had happened, and there were those who thought it would be a long time before Younger reëstablished his credit with him.

Acting very much like a man who had made a promise that *he* meant to keep, Harris immediately took the floor. "Are we going to take the position, shall we say, that a doctor is going to practice medicine and determine what drugs to prescribe for anyone by reading an advertisement in the *Journal* of the American Medical Association or a state medical journal or magazine?" he demanded. "Is that what you are going to say to the people of this country?"

Dingell had been waiting for this. Rising quickly, he quoted an A.M.A. study to the effect that doctors were greatly alarmed by "a company knowingly misleading the doctor through bad advertising." Dingell continued, "According to the survey, this is accomplished in three ways. First, by 'exaggerated product claims.' Second, by 'releasing news on a drug to the medical profession before it has been fully tested.' And, third—the worst of all—'advertising the advantages of a drug without mentioning its side effects.' On this last point, the survey had found, ninety per cent of the doctors consider it 'the most heinous crime a pharmaceutical company can commit.'" In conclusion, he drew attention to another specific drug. "You have all heard about Norlutin," he said. "It was a substance which was marketed and made available to mothers. This substance created male hermaphroditism in female infants. Three months after this fact was found and was reported on in a circular to the medical profession, the manufacturer's ads were still proclaiming the safety of Norlutin."

As Dingell took his seat, Harris happened to look around, and saw that the chamber had almost filled up, largely with members of the Democratic Study Group, a hundred of whom had responded to the two whip calls—an unprecedented turnout. "You could see Harris cave in physically," said one congressman who had been sitting near him. "His eyes flickered back and forth over the audience, and then, when he realized who most of the newcomers were, his shoulders sagged. He knew that he'd had it." Just then a cluster of liberals who wanted to make the most of the opportune moment began chanting "Vote! Vote! Vote! Vote!" and at that Harris agreed to accept Blatnik's amendment, provided one change was made—the addition of a statement that side effects could be described in advertisements "in brief summary." This was a change that Dingell had proposed to him as a face-saving way out. A few minutes later, a voice vote was taken on Blatnik's amendment, and it won resoundingly.

Just after the vote, Blair, who was sitting in the gallery, turned to see how Corcoran, Foley, and Cutler were taking it. "They looked like statues on Easter Island," he said afterward. In the corridor outside the gallery, Sonosky sagged against a wall, grinning broadly. "Boy, I feel good," he said. "I really feel good." Suddenly, the gallery door opened, and Corcoran brushed past him without a glance. "We beat you!" Sonosky muttered as he passed, and grinned again. On the House floor, Dingell was surrounded by some members of the Study Group, who were congratulating him. "I'm so happy I'm just bursting," he said. "It's a great victory for the public interest."

The rest of the bill took little time to consider, and at ten minutes after five the House, by another voice vote, approved it unanimously, whereupon the members burst into spontaneous applause—an unusual demonstration that led a veteran member of the House press corps to remark, "I guess they must be applauding themselves. It's not often they're able to do something for the people." As Albert Jay Nock wrote of legislative bodies in general, "They sometimes do a good thing, but never do one merely because it is a good thing."

XVII The penultimate act in the legislative process is the Senate-House conference to adjust differences between bills on the same matter that have been passed by both. The Speaker of the House appoints the House conferees—or the bill's managers, as they are officially referred to—and the presiding officer of the Senate appoints the Senate conferees, but in practice they merely accept recommendations made by the chairmen of the committees that have considered the two bills. The proponents of a strong drug bill feared that Harris might appoint a battery of conservatives from his committee, for it was reported that the industry still had hopes of getting its way in conference. However, he followed tradition by choosing as conferees, in addition to himself, members of his committee's Subcommittee on Health and Safety: Democrats Kenneth A. Roberts, Leo W. O'Brien, and Paul G. Rogers, of Alabama, New York, and Florida, respectively, and Republicans Bennett, Paul F. Schenck, of Ohio, and Ancher Nelsen, of Minnesota. Eastland did things differently: He followed seniority in the full committee rather than in the Subcommittee on Antitrust and Monopoly, with the result that Dirksen and Hruska were selected to represent the Republicans, while he picked Kefauver (who was outranked only by Eastland) and Johnston (who was not even on the subcommittee), thus passing over Hart, the bill's co-sponsor, and Carroll, both of whom had attended more of the drug hearings than any other members of the subcommittee except Kefauver and Hruska.

At two-thirty on the afternoon of October 1st, the conferees met in a room in the newly extended East Front of the Capitol, halfway between the Senate and House chambers. Because Harris had been taken to the hospital that morning for an operation, he had turned over his position as head of the committee to Roberts, the chairman of the Subcommittee on Health and Safety, who was a fairly consistent liberal. Johnston was also absent, and had given his proxy to Eastland. Throughout the day, the corridor outside was populated by most of the lobbyists, a few Senate staff members, and Sonosky, Ellenbogen, and Rankin. Their wait did them no good, for when the meeting broke up at dinnertime, nothing was announced; it was known only that the conferees had not yet got to the advertising amendment. Eastland had clamped a tight security lid on the proceedings to avert the kind of publicity that had brought down the Younger amendment, it was said—but apparently the industry people on hand were excluded, for he and Hruska walked off with the top three P.M.A. strategists, while several of the House conferees left with two or three lobbyists each. Kefauver was the last man out of the room, and he departed alone.

That night, Dingell received word that the industry had prepared a new version of the advertising amendment, which was almost identical to Younger's. The next morning, he hurried over to the conference room before the meeting convened, and told the House members who had arrived that if they reneged on the Blatnik amendment, he would take the House floor and make Blatnik's job on Younger look like a compliment.

The conference resumed at ten o'clock, without Eastland, Dirksen, and Johnston. The riots at the University of Mississippi, which had broken out on September 30th, were occupying Eastland, and he had told Kefauver the evening before that neither he nor Johnston, who was also busy, would be present at the next day's session, and had added, "I trust that you'll look after our interests." To Kefauver, this seemed an unexpected break, giving him two votes that he might not otherwise have been able to count on. Dirksen, whose duties as Minority Leader kept him away, had given his vote to Hruska. The first item on the agenda was the new advertising amendment. It was offered by Hruska, and provoked a long and bitter debate. Because the House members, for the most part, were unfamiliar with the intricacies of the two bills, Hruska was able to develop a number of arguments in favor of the new amendment, but Kefauver quickly countered each of them with facts and figures that brought the representatives around to his point of view.

"When you first sit down with Kefauver, you think you're dealing with a pushover," Congressman O'Brien said later that day. "At the start, I thought that Hruska, who is an incisive, aggressive fellow, would murder him, but it just didn't happen that way. Kefauver was extremely knowledgeable, and, in his own quiet way, extremely tough. He picked a good position and stayed there—as if his feet were planted in the ground. That made Hruska jump all over the place."

Sonosky and Rankin, who had seen the new amendment and realized that Hruska would win if he could swing a couple of House votes to his side, went to work on a compromise proposal to avert this. When they had finished it, Sonosky sent a note into the conference room asking Blair to step outside for a moment. A minute later, Blair appeared, read the substitute quickly, shook his head in curt dismissal, and, without a word, walked back to the door. A little later, Sonosky, despite Blair's opposition, showed the substitute to Cutler, who thereupon called out Raitt, Hruska's assistant. These two studied the proposal and discussed it at some length, and then went over to Sonosky.

"Can we say that this compromise is acceptable to H.E.W.?" Raitt asked.

"Well, I wouldn't put it that way," Sonosky answered after some thought. "If it's acceptable to Kefauver and the

House, we won't oppose it. After all, as the original sponsor, Kefauver deserves *some* consideration."

Once Raitt had returned to the conference room, Sonosky dashed off a note on legal paper to Kefauver, saying, in part, "This is a reasonable amendment that F.D.A. says would not restrict their enforcement powers in any respect. As a retreat position from Senator Hruska's amendment it could be termed 'acceptable' without weakening the bill."

A moment later, Fensterwald came out of the conference room and walked over to Sonosky. "What in the name of God do you think you're doing?" he demanded. "Don't you realize that your readiness to compromise, no matter how you phrase it, weakens Kefauver's hand? Why should we back down before we have to?"

Twice that morning, Hruska proposed the P.M.A. amendment, only to be beaten off by Kefauver and the House members, who, though they wavered from time to time, ultimately held fast. In each instance, the situation was not entirely clear, so Hruska, apparently not wanting to risk anything until he was more certain of the outcome, held off from calling for a vote, and the conferees went on to other matters. In the course of these deliberations, Kefauver managed to get approval for several provisions that had been left out of the House bill, including a requirement that new drugs be tested on animals before they were tested on human beings, a requirement that Health, Education, and Welfare review and be authorized to simplify generic names, a requirement that all drug manufacturers register with the government, and permission for Health, Education, and Welfare to furnish information on new drugs to the Patent Office. Also, he took the initiative in changing the so-called patient-consent provision so that it was no longer mandatory, as it had been in the House bill, for a doctor to get a release from a patient before treating him with a new, unapproved drug, provided that, in the physician's best judgment, securing a release would not be in the patient's best interest or was not feasible. However, Kefauver failed to get amendments providing that package inserts on all drugs be sent to doctors throughout the country, and that animal antibiotics be included under the certification rule. (This failure, he said later, would mean that inferior antibiotics could now be dumped in animal feed.) Kefauver employed his usual strategy; that is, when he did not accomplish what he wanted on a first try, he would go on to something else and then come back, time and again, to the matter in question.

Finally, Hruska complained, "If we go on this way, we'll be here until Christmas. I think that may be what Senator Kefauver wants anyway."

Kefauver turned to him, smiled, and said calmly, "Why, Roman, that's ridiculous." However, realizing that his opponents would like nothing better than to see the bill stalled under conditions that could be blamed on him, he then agreed to a couple of minor compromises.

After a break for lunch, Hruska brought up the new advertising amendment for a third time, having meanwhile obtained the support of Congressman Schenck. Although Kefauver did not care for the phrase "in brief summary," which constituted the one difference between the Senate and House advertising amendments, he decided, now that one House member had championed the P.M.A. amendment, to accept the House version. Saying as much, he faced the congressmen across the table and asked, "How can you reject your own bill?"

Hruska argued that they could if they found its language

unsuitable. A moment later, Hruska proposed still another advertising amendment, and when Kefauver fought that, too, objecting that in reality it was the same as the other, Hruska stopped him with a wave of the hand. "This is the wish of the Senate," he said. With a surprised look, Kefauver said, "Wait a minute. It's not *my* wish as a member of the Senate."

Hruska then played his trump card: he had all three proxies—Dirksen's, Eastland's, and Johnston's—and therefore, by a vote of four to one, it was the wish of the Senate. Kefauver stared at him openmouthed for a moment, and then said that Eastland had given him his and Johnston's proxies the night before, whereupon Hruska smiled once more and replied that Eastland had given *him* their proxies that morning. Kefauver, still dazed by Eastland's move, sat stunned.

At that moment, Congressman Roberts, who was serving as chairman of the conference, spoke up. "Senator Hruska, what you ask is impossible," he said. "We simply cannot go back to the House with a different amendment. We *know* what would happen to us on the floor. It's out of the question to even consider it."

Hruska looked inquiringly at Schenck, but Schenck averted his eyes. It was now clear to Hruska that even with the three proxies he didn't have the necessary support, and he conceded without bothering to call for a vote.

"We felt that the House committee had made a mistake on the Younger amendment by then," Congressman O'Brien said later, "and we were happy to cut it out. Also, the thalidomide scandal had proved that Kefauver had been right all along. That meant he started out with three aces as far as the House members were concerned. And then his reputation as a strong public-interest man had a great effect on us. In the end, Kefauver proved that you can't count one vote for one man. It all depends on the man's weight."

Shortly after Hruska's final defeat on the advertising amendment, the conference came to an end. Although Kefauver was still outraged by the proxy deal—and later told Eastland as much—he was delighted with the outcome. "We've come up with a good strong bill," he told reporters.

If it did nothing about prices, the bill was far better and stronger than he had hoped for—even at the start.

Congressman Roberts described the new bill to the reporters and lobbyists, who filed into the room after the meeting adjourned. The industry men looked at Roberts in disbelief as he went on, for the bill that had come out of conference was, in sum, stronger than either of those that had gone in. Soon afterward, the lobbyists, still looking rather dazed, straggled out of the room. If they were cast down by the drug bill, they were soon to get more heartening news, for that afternoon Congress passed a new tax bill; buried in it was a provision making lobbyists' expenses deductible. According to the New York *Times*, an industry spokesman had estimated that the "out-of-pocket costs to be met in refuting the Kefauver charges" had come to five million dollars. Over the four-year period from the start of the drug investigation to the passage of the bill, the Subcommittee on Antitrust and Monopoly had spent some three hundred thousand dollars on its work in the drug field.

XVIII

In an election year, Congress looks forward to adjournment in much the same way that mailmen, around the first of December, look forward to the day after Christmas. In both lines of work, the end of the rush means getting back down to one's real business. During the second session of the Eighty-seventh Congress, the administration had dropped so many bills into the congressional mailbox that it looked for a time as if the members might have to remain in Washington right up to Election Eve. More often than not in such years, Congress adjourns in August, but in 1962 the session dragged on into October. Those who had to face their constituents at the polls the following month talked increasingly about decamping whether or not their work was finished. Kefauver was particularly unsettled by such remarks, for, of course, no uncompleted bill survives the Congress in which it is introduced. Although he was confident that enough time remained to get the drug bill through the Senate, he was not at all sure about its fate in the House. First, he had to wait while the conference report was printed up, and then he faced a delay created by a rule of Congress stipulating that one house could not vote on a conference report until forty-eight hours after it had been approved by the other. Since all the members of the House were up for reëlection, the restiveness there over the inordinate length of the session was far more ominous than anything to be encountered in the Senate, where only a third of the members had campaigns to wage. Moreover, Kefauver remembered that in 1954 the House had got so tired of waiting for the Senate to adjourn that it had simply packed up and gone home. To expedite matters, he first prevailed on the Government Printing Office to prepare the conference report overnight, then persuaded Mansfield to put it on the agenda for the next day, and, finally, got him to arrange for a suspension of the forty-eight-hour rule.

Eastland, who was still preoccupied with the University

of Mississippi riots, turned the job of managing the conference report, which included delivering a speech about the bill on the floor, over to Kefauver. Kefauver was delighted at this, for it gave him an opportunity to contribute further to the legislative history of the bill. At four-thirty on the morning of October 3rd, Blair went to work on the Senator's speech. As each page was typed, it was taken in to Kefauver, who made corrections and revisions. It was ready by mid-afternoon, and Kefauver and Blair went over to the Senate. As they sat in the Senate chamber waiting for Mansfield to give the signal that it was time for Kefauver to take the floor, Blair mulled over the speech, which was a highly detailed document, without a dash of either drama or political philosophy, and finally said to Kefauver, "You know, Estes, this is a pretty dry way of ending things after all these years and all this struggle. You really ought to have something a little grander to wind it up."

Kefauver agreed, and after some discussion, he and Blair came up with an idea for a peroration. When Mansfield gave Kefauver the nod, he got up and droned on for an hour about the specific purposes of the bill. When he finally got to the end, he faced the presiding officer. "In conclusion, Mr. President," he said, again raising his voice, "this bill constitutes something of a tribute to the Founding Fathers for their wisdom in creating the legislative branch as a separate branch of government. The separation of the legislative from the executive branch has long been criticized by proponents of the parliamentary form of government. But I doubt whether under a parliamentary system the investigation [of the drug industry] would ever have been made [or] new and original remedies conceived. . . . This was not one of the all too frequent situations in which the role of Congress was merely that of passing upon a proposal developed by the executive branch, nor did it involve merely taking an old bill which had been rejected, updating it, and inserting some new touches to make it current. The bill involved new thinking, new ideas. They came from a legislative committee. At the outset of the investigation, we were actually discouraged by top officials of the Food and Drug Administration. Not only had they no remedies for most of the problems with which we were beginning to be concerned; they did not even recognize them as problems. . . . The moral of the drug bill is that even on an exceedingly complex issue the legislative branch can perform in the manner originally intended [by the framers of the Constitution]. With only a small staff of competent professional personnel, the Congress can prove itself to be just as able as the vast bureacracy of the executive branch, if not more so, to assume leadership in the legislative process."

A few minutes later, the conference report was approved by the Senate without dissent. Soon after that, Hruska rose to have his final say. Addressing the chair, which was then occupied by Senator Neuberger, he smiled and said, "Madam President, this is an instance in which we can well apply the old proverb or classical saying that 'all's well that ends well.' The bill before us is a good bill. It is sound and workable. It is acceptable to those who will be in charge of its administration and enforcement, and it is acceptable to industry. Most of all, it is very acceptable to the public, which has the greatest stake of all." However, he went on, just to keep the record straight, he wanted to point out that, "with one exception and some small refinements," the bill was little different from the Eastland-Dirksen bill of July 19th. "The efforts leading up to the introduction in this chamber of the bill of July 19th were of no small moment," he continued. "They were in keeping with the highest legislative traditions." Then, taking one last pot shot at Kefauver, he said, "On several occasions, it appeared that no bill would be forthcoming. At those critical times, the efforts of the Chairman of the Committee on the Judiciary and of the Senator from Illinois were a particularly steadying influence. Had it not been for them, progress might have come to a standstill, and success not been attained."

Across the aisle, Senator Dodd rose to speak his piece. "I have an idea that the Senator from Tennessee will be remembered long after all of us in this chamber at this hour are gone for the many great things he has accomplished," he said. "I cannot think of anything better I would wish to have said about me in this body than . . . that I was at his side in this battle, and in others as well."

Shortly after one-thirty the following afternoon, the House approved the conference report unanimously. "The hero of this victory," the *Times* noted in an editorial, "is Senator Kefauver of Tennessee, who doggedly continued to push for this needed legislation despite widespread public apathy, lack of administration interest and bitter opposition from some industry and Congressional sources."

President Kennedy was scheduled to sign the act on October 10th, but the morning of the ninth came and went without Kefauver's receiving an invitation to attend the signing. That afternoon, his staff urged him to force the issue by calling Feldman, but Kefauver refused. They continued to press the matter, though, and finally the Senator put down a dog-eared copy of *How to Win Friends and Influence People,* which he had been rereading after several years, and told his secretary to call Feldman. Upon being put through, he asked who was going to be at the ceremony. Feldman quickly invited him, and went on to say that so far no one had been asked but that the plans were to include a number of members of Congress, including Dirksen. Kefauver said, "My God, the Republicans fought us every inch of the way. Why give them public praise? I'd rather there was no ceremony at all."

Upon entering the White House the next morning, Kefauver found that his objection had been heeded. On hand, besides the President and Kefauver himself, were Dr. Kelsey, Commissioner Larrick, Senators Hart, Humphrey, and Johnston, and Representatives Roberts and O'Brien. The ceremony got under way at a little before ten o'clock and lasted only a few minutes. President Kennedy put the first pen (an Esterbrook, inscribed "The President–The White House") to the document, now designated Public Law 87-781; he wrote part of his signature, and then stopped and looked around. After a brief pause, he handed the pen to Kefauver. "Here, you played the most important part, Estes, so you get the first pen," he said. With an embarrassed smile, Senator Kefauver took the pen and looked at it as if he were slightly surprised. A moment later, collecting himself, he said, "Thank you, Mr. President."